DISCIPLINE FOR GREATNESS

FIVE SIMPLE STEPS TO SUCCESS & HAPPINESS

by

JOEY PINZ

LEADERSHIP
BOOKS

DISCIPLINE FOR GREATNESS
By JOEY PINZ

Copyright 2025
Publisher: Leadership Books, Inc.
Las Vegas, Nevada, and New York, New York.

All rights reserved. This book is protected under the copyright laws of the United States of America This book may not be copied or reprinted for commercial gain or profit. No part of this publication may be reproduced, distributed, or transmitted in any form or by any means, including photocopying, recording, or other electronic or mechanical methods, without the prior written permission of the publisher, except in the case of brief quotations embodied in critical reviews and certain the use of short quotations or occasional page copying for personal, or group study is permitted and encouraged. Permission will be granted upon request.

Hardcover: 978-1-965401-06-4
Paperback: 978-1-965401-07-1
eBook: 978-1-965401-14-9

For Worldwide Distribution

DEDICATION

Why write a book about Discipline? It continues to be the foundation of all my success and happiness. My friends and colleagues insisted that I write down how I used Discipline in my life. The fundamental reason for starting the podcast was to discover how discipline plays a role in lives.

I dedicate this book to those who find it difficult to complete their goals. Use Discipline, focus, and routine to plan and achieve your goals.

I dedicate this book to those who want to find happiness. Create a plan to achieve happiness and use Discipline to get there.

Do you need to lose weight? Don't wait to hit rock bottom like I did to make it happen. Use Discipline and make it a priority.

Do you need to be a better business, family, or community leader? Use this book to create a plan and manage it with Discipline.

There is no greater satisfaction than seeing friends, colleagues, or acquaintances succeed and do well. If I played a + .0000001 percent in that success, that's all the better. The methods and processes in this book are what I use to achieve. Please take all or parts of the book to make you happy and succeed! Good people do things for other people.

"A society grows great when old men plant trees the shade of which they will never sit."

– Greek Proverb

ACKNOWLEDGMENTS

The podcasting world is an interesting one. With minimum barriers of entry, I have found that there are many podcasts, but no real community. Most podcasts stop before the 10th episode, dreaming of being the next Joe Rogan and making millions of dollars. Therefore, many transients come and go.

When I made my business plan for my Joey Pinz Podcast, the Mission and Vision were and continue to be:

- Mission—How do we use Discipline to better ourselves and society?
- Vision—Growth through learning from others

Revenue is low on my priority list. I have the benefit of having many resources due to my successful businesses. I can schedule time, automate processes through the experience of my tech company, and hire virtual assistants to do many tasks.

I have turned down many sponsors for the podcast because I didn't think it was a fit.

On a whim, I went to a local podcast event when given a free ticket by one of the podcast platforms we subscribe to.

I was very skeptical, given that I am used to tech conferences and understand the rhythm and temperament of people in my profession. With podcasters being such an eclectic group, I had no idea what to expect. I am an ambivert, an extrovert when I want to be, and an introvert at other times.

The event was great. The people were amiable, and the sessions were informative.

Many of the podcast speakers had written books. There was an Author's Row, where the authors displayed their books and were open for discussion. Some authors wrote their books, then started a podcast, and others created it first. Authors and podcasters seemed to have a direct correlation.

Years ago, I considered writing a book, contacted some publishers and ghostwriters, and got very frustrated with the reception and unclean nature of the promises and advice.

In speaking to these podcast authors, I began considering writing a book on Discipline. I have been crafting a methodology based on Discipline knowing it.

There were many book publishing companies at this podcast event. I spoke to many of them. Remember that I did not attend this event to write a book. I attended to get a taste of the podcast community and decide what role I wanted to play.

In speaking to the book publishers, I began to understand the difference. Most organizations would help write the book for the writer to self-publish. After long thought and review, I decided I did not want to be in the book-selling business.

I wanted to write the book and have a team work with me to edit, shape, market, and sell. I decided to go with a publisher.

I always found writing difficult. I love to speak in public. I am a much better communicator at speaking than I am writing. I can write down my thoughts in a stream of consciousness. The act of editing is very time-consuming. I love Mark Twain's quote apologizing to his sister for writing a long letter: "I didn't have time to write a short letter, so I wrote a long one instead." I am a better editor than I am a writer.

With guidance and direction from the team, I got the first draft in about a month. I really enjoyed the process and will do it again.

I thank my close family and friends for supporting me on this journey. No one tried to talk me out of this journey. They all said something to the effect of, "Yeah, that makes sense, Joe. I can see you as a published author."

The man who loves walking will walk further than the man who loves the destination.

ACKNOWLEDGMENTS

I have several inspirations when it comes to interviewing style and conversation. In no order, **I would like to acknowledge and give tribute to the following listed friends:** I'll put the order alphabetically. They all mean a lot to me, so much so that I mentioned them thusly.

RON BENNINGTON

Ron Bennington is an American radio personality and comedian who is currently the co-host of Bennington and host of Unmasked. He has also been a co-host of other radio shows: The Ron and Ron Show and The Ron and Fez Show with Fez Whatley. He started his career as a stand-up comedian and comedy club owner and promoter. He is known for his witty, street-smart, and sarcastic humor.

Ron conducts incredibly strong interviews with celebrities and comedians. Ron, justifiably, has a large and loyal fan base. I have been listening to Ron Bennington for ten-plus years. He is unquestionably the most consistently funny, enjoyable, and professional host ever.

Ron's current show on XM Radio is a must-listen. I have not missed an episode for a long time. While not listening live all of the time, I catch up on the reruns. He is a genuinely hilarious person to the bone. His interest in the arts, music, film, food, and comedy is inspirational.

Fez Whatley, a now-deceased former host, was a wonderful human being. A perfect yin to Ron's yang. He would make me laugh for hours. I have met Fez twice, furthering my belief that he was a genuinely wonderful human being. I miss you, Mr. Whatley.

Ron conducts a separate "unmasked" series where he interviews people, one individually, with a tiny audience. I have participated in a few of these, which are spectacular. His homework and general interest in the person and their work are astounding. How he relates to his guests and puts them at ease is lovely to behold.

I met Ron several times, which meant the world to me. He continues to be an inspiration. Now hosting with his daughter Gayle, his show takes a splendid turn. We see Ron as a grandfather, and he has never been better. His vulnerability, still with an incredibly humorous foundation, is spectacular to behold.

I simply think Ron is the best interviewer I have ever witnessed.

I once spoke to Penn Jillette after one of the Penn and Teller shows in Las Vegas. This was just after the release of his book *God, No!*. Ron had just interviewed him weeks before. The first thing I said to him was I enjoyed the Ron Bennington interview. His reply was that Ron is the best interview ever.

After releasing my podcast, I was interviewed on the Bennington Show. One day Ron commented on the podcast and applauded my ability with, "He is a good interview." Wow!

I recorded it and saved it. Perhaps the highest praise I could ever receive. I generally don't like to hear compliments or complaints, but this is undoubtedly an exception.

I don't know anyone that listens to or knows Ron Bennington or his show. I tell people about it, but I will attest that he is the greatest.

JOE ROGAN

Joe Rogan is an American podcaster, comedian, UFC color commentator, martial arts instructor, actor, and television presenter. The biggest podcast in the world is the JRE, Joe Rogan Experience. I remember listening to Joe on the Opie and Anthony show. He was always fascinating and introspective. I had heard he had something called a podcast but was unsure about it.

I eventually became a fan of the JRE. Joe and the JRE is responsible for so much positivity in my life. I call it the Joe Rogan Experience Effect or the J R double E. There are many changes I have made through listening to the JRE with the incredible guests he has interviewed.

ACKNOWLEDGMENTS

Joe's guests have amazed me. I have watched so many documentaries from directors and creators he has had on. I have been exposed to so many points of view from MMA, hunting, diet, cold plunge, stretching, exercising, mental fitness, comedy, history, science, and everything in between.

Joe does not get enough credit for how great a host he is. He drives all of that conversation for three-plus hours. As an interviewer, I can see how prepared he is and how he navigates the conversation in so many directions. Here are a few topics:

Supplements: The many health experts he has on makes me take daily supplements, including Quercetin, lion's mane, fish oil, vitamin D, E, and a multivitamin.

Martial Arts: While I am very new, I see the beautiful effects of self-discipline and calmness from martial arts. Joe is a black belt in multiple martial arts, and it reflects in his mannerisms.

Political Homelessness: I cannot relate to politics. It's very polarizing and always has been. We are good, they are wrong. It's all a money game to me. I have some liberal beliefs as well as some conservative beliefs. It comes down to power and money with politics, which is boring to me.

Openness. Don't dig in. Listen. I love hearing the guest's perspective. Even if it is different from mine. Given new credible evidence, I reserve the right to change my mind on any particular topic. Imagine how. much better the world would be if we all adopted this philosophy.

Starting a Podcast: There was a while when Joe was convincing guests to start podcasts. Let people hear your voice. Perhaps with more than three million listeners, Joe has curbed that, but he is the main reason I started my podcast.

Joe spent his high school years in Massachusetts, near me in Connecticut. I relate to his high school stories. He was a bouncer at a popular concert venue where I attended many shows. While I have never met Mr. Rogan, I look forward to one day, and perhaps even having him on the podcast, as I admire and respect him greatly.

CHARLIE ROSE

Charlie Rose is an American former television journalist and talk show host. He is best known for hosting Charlie Rose, a TV interview and talk show that ran from 1991 to 2017 on PBS and Bloomberg. He also co-anchored CBS This Morning from 2012 to 2017 alongside Gayle King and Norah O'Donnell. He has interviewed many celebrities and world leaders, such as Barack Obama, Bill Gates, Oprah Winfrey, and Vladimir Putin.

During college, I would be up late at night doing who knows what. Charlie Rose would come on sometime after David Letterman. I was astounded how Charlie could make someone I had never heard of so interesting.

I would listen for the whole hour with a Russian ballerina, Irish politician, actor, writer, or director. That black room with the round brown table was captivating. Charlie, with his Carolina accent, would steer the conversation masterfully. He wanted to get to the root of a particular subject, and felt it during the conversation there. His paper notes that he would never seem to reference showed his classic style and preparedness.

I learned that everyone has a story. Not just celebrities, but everyone has a story. One-on-one deep conversations with interesting people for me started with Charlie Rose.

LEX FRIDMAN

Lex Fridman is a Russian-American computer scientist, podcaster, and an artificial intelligence researcher. He is a research scientist at MIT and he hosts the Lex Fridman Podcast, a podcast and YouTube series about science, technology, history, philosophy, and more.

His Rod Serling-type style, whether intentionally or not, is compelling, sincere and warm.

His eagerness to learn more from his guests is inspiring. He prepares brilliantly and can incorporate his tech AI knowledge and other fascinating sources into the conversations. I was introduced to Lex from the Joe Rogan Experience Podcast.

You would think his academic background would not lend to a beautiful improvising conversation, but it does. He has many handwritten notes on paper that he references often. Not always looking into the guest's eyes, he asks thought-provoking deep questions and yearns for their answers.

His approach to conversation is unique and admirable. I so enjoy his conversations. He is not afraid to ask hard questions. Often self-deprecating and humble, he lifts the viewer's attention and invites the guest to open up and be themselves. I have never met Lex, but I hope to one day.

HOW CAN I HELP?

Nobody asks this question anymore. It's a straightforward but powerful question. It opens the one asking to a vulnerable place. Sometimes replaced with "How can I help you?" adding emphasis to the question in particular is even more empowering.

I am not talking about a clerk at a store or a receptionist on the phone who simply rattles off how I can help as If it's part of their job. I'm talking about a genuine How can I help you? What can I do to make things better in your life? I am not obligated to respond to their request if it is outrageous and selfish. But just asking the question lowers the guardedness of the person asked.

I often ask friends when they present a problem or issue if I could solve their problem with a simple call, email, or light effort? I use this often, and many times people are put off guard. They are not used to hearing this, so they don't know how to react. Most of the time, I don't get an answer. But just letting a friend or colleague know that you have asked if you can help makes all the difference.

Many times, I wish someone had told me how I could help. Just to listen, hug, or sit for a meal. Let's engage in a conversation. Now there may be examples where someone may take this too far and ask too much. Yet this has never happened to me. I would handle it accordingly, as you are not under any obligation.

It's almost like when someone gives you advice. There are those who give you advice, then don't take it. Advice is voluntary, not compulsory. Asking how to help is similar. I have had one friend say, "Yes, help me." When I responded, it became obvious they just wanted to talk and vent and were not interested in a solution or in any help.

But that's not me. I truly want to help like my esteemed colleagues acknowledged above helped me. My hope and desire is that this book will help you, and that's why I've written this book.

TABLE OF CONTENTS

Introduction .... *xxi*

CHAPTER 1: Life Disciplines 1
   Personal *2*
   Family *3*
   Professional *8*
   Community *9*

CHAPTER 2: Discipline is a Spectrum 13
   1-Focus *39*
   2-Restraint *50*
   3-Obedience *62*
   4-Mastery *69*
   5-Control *76*
   6-Routine *89*
   7-Order *98*
   8-Willpower *104*
   9-Direction *111*
   10-Strictness *118*

CHAPTER 3: 5 steps to success and happiness 135
   Step 01 Define Success *145*
   Step 02 Identify, Strengths, Passions and Disciplines ... *165*
   Step 03 Plan: create specific deadlines and Actions ... *183*
   Step 04 Iterate and Repeat *209*
   Step 05 Balance Life Disciplines *213*

Bibliography *217*
Conclusion *279*
Bio *281*

PREFACE

Many people say this, "If I can lose weight, anyone can." Losing weight is one of the most challenging things to do in life. It takes Discipline! And losing weight is only the first part of the journey. Keeping it off is perhaps the most challenging part. Close to 90 percent of people who lose dramatic amounts of weight gain it back. Perhaps they feel since they did it once, they can do it again.

Losing weight takes a life shift. It's not a temporary fix. One must change their relationship to the three main pillars of health: Diet, Exercise, and Sleep.

Starting a business takes many levels of Discipline. When I started my tech firm in 1993, I was skeptical. Ninety-five percent of small businesses fail in the first year. I persevered and made it through. To be a business owner, one must have focus, routine, and all the other characteristics of Discipline.

At the time of this writing, there were more than three million podcasts. I started the Joey Pinz Podcast in September of 2021. I created a business plan and attacked the podcast like any other business. I have interviewed hundreds of impressive people about their success and made a point to ask every guest how Discipline plays a role in their life.

I say this humbly. I am not an extraordinary person. I just work hard and try to learn from my failures.

I was convinced to write this book to help those achieve success and happiness.

All of the evidence is purely anecdotal. We derived this from our own experiences, and from the guests on the podcast. There is always room for improvement. Happiness is amazing. It's so amazing it doesn't matter if it's yours or not. Good luck on your journey. I hope I can help you!

JOEY PINZ DISCIPLINE CONVERSATIONS PODCAST—VIDEO AND AUDIO

Podcasts by definition have been audio content. Many podcasts, including the Joey Pinz podcast, include video that can be downloaded or streamed online. Podcast episodes generally focus on a topic or theme, such as music, education, comedy, sports, or music. Podcasts have become increasingly popular, with millions of listeners around the world. But there's one theme that makes every Joey Pinz Discipline my Podcast currency.

Multitasking is a major reason why podcasts are popular. Unlike watching TV or reading a book, listening to a podcast does not require full attention. Someone can listen to podcasts while doing other things, like, exercising, driving, or gardening. This saves time and makes activities more enjoyable. According to Edison Research, most people listen to podcasts at home (49 percent), in a car (22 percent), while walking around (11 percent), or working out (4 percent).

The popularity of podcasts is also because they cover niche topics. Mainstream media outlets that tend to focus on broad and general topics, podcasts can cater to specific interests and passions of listeners. Podcasts can be on any topic from murder mystery to basketball to sewing. Giving access to diverse perspectives and insights that are not found elsewhere.

People can listen to podcasts on their own schedule, whenever and wherever they would like. You can also choose from a variety of platforms and devices that suit your preferences. Podcasts can be educational, informative, entertaining, and engrossing. They can make you think, learn, cry, laugh, or feel inspired by their content and design. Podcasts can also connect you with like-minded communities and foster a sense of belonging among listeners who share similar interests or ideals.

Podcasts are common because they provide many benefits for modern listeners who value multitasking, specialty topics, accessibility, and leisure. Podcasts are flexible and available in audio, and video content that appeals to diverse audiences. At the time of this writing, there are approximately three million podcasts. Approximately 50 percent are less than ten episodes, and 7 percent do not last more than a year.

We were spending my 52nd birthday in Breckenridge. Someone made the comment that I ask a lot of questions. I have always been a fan of question-based learning. When I want to understand something, I ask questions. Seems pretty simple. Some have said I have been a bit interrogative, so I try to monitor and be aware this.

Socrates is the founder and creator of the Socratic method. He invented question-based learning. When asking an AI engine what the Socratic method is:

> The Socratic method is a form of philosophical inquiry that uses a series of questions to lead the person being questioned to a deeper understanding of a topic or concept. It is named after the ancient Greek philosopher Socrates, who is known for his use of this method in his teaching and conversations with others. In the Socratic method, the teacher asks questions encouraging the student to critically examine their ideas and beliefs. This involves questioning their thinking and challenging their hypotheses. The goal is not to impose a particular point of view but rather to encourage the person being questioned to arrive at their own conclusions through reasoned inquiry and reflection.

I learned in college that it was Socrates who invented this, and I have employed his technique for most of my life. I love talking to people who do exciting things. Even better, talking to people that have overcome immense obstacles.

I remember asking a artist in Breckenridge who was selling her work:

- When did you receive inspiration to paint this?
- Did you get inspiration from something else?
- When you got this inspiration, did you have to run to the canvas and get it out before losing it?
- Did you envision this entire painting or just parts?

- Did all the colors come to you before or during the painting?
- How long did it take?
- When completed, was it exactly how you envisioned it?
- Does it matter what others think of it?
- Does it bother you when others don't see the same thing you see in it?

There may have been more questions than listed above, but she answered them all attentively. It was a wonderful conversation. I also mentioned how I overcame losing a lot of weight, and when asked how, my reply is always Discipline.

How does Discipline play a role in your life was only a natural question.

It was after this that I knew I needed to start a podcast. On September 1, 2022, the Joey Pinz Discipline Conversation dropped. I have recorded hundreds of episodes with people in the following categories only to eventually ask each of them, "How Discipline plays a role in their life?"

- **Health, Fitness, Sports & Wellness:**
  - WeightLoss
  - Exercise, Fitness & Athletics
  - EatingHealthy & Diet
  - Jiu-Jitsu and martialarts
  - Relationships
  - Golf and soccer
- **Business, Technology & Science:**
  - Business Growth
  - Productivity and Process
  - Empowerment
  - Sales and marketing
- **Art & Culture:**
  - Expanding taste & curiosity in: Food, Travel, Film, Music and Comedy

PREFACE

My style of interview, or a conversation, is to ask questions and listen. As I get older, I find I have more questions than answers. Ask questions and listen. I see too many podcast hosts not listening. Waiting to speak is very different from listening.

I do my homework. I study about my guests. I am fully prepared for the conversation. I look for answers in my discovery and prepare my questions.

It's not about the host. When I have a conversation on the podcast, it's about the guest. No one cares about me or the show. They want to find out more about the guest I selected to be there.

"Hey, welcome to my show. This is my tenth episode, and I am sitting on the beach!" Who cares! Also, don't ask the guest to introduce themselves. It all comes off as lazy to me.

As soon as we record, I ask my first question. Let's get this thing going!

I remember Jerry Seinfeld talking about this with stand-up comedy. He was saying how many comics start off with their feelings or what kind of coffee they like. Jerry says, get right into it. You are paid to be there. Start working! I share Mr. Seinfeld's attitude on this topic.

Another thing I find annoying with some podcasts is how they over-sensationalize what is happening. They say, "Here is my first question… 'How did you get here.'" Why announce it's your first question? Make it a real conversation, not an interview. A real conversation does not say things like that.

Be sincere and curious about their answers. Make it real, people. This is my way. Other great podcasts do it differently, but I prefer it this way. After all, the podcast is for me, and everyone else is just invited.

I never ask what listeners would want to hear or ask. I ask what I am interested in and welcome all to witness. I want the podcast to feel organic and genuine because, it is.

Quentin Tarantino has a great philosophy about his movies—he creates films that he likes and wants to watch, inviting others to enjoy them as well. Rick Rubin holds a similar belief with the music he produces. I've adopted this mindset for my conversations: I am genuine, asking questions that I truly want answers to, and I invite others to watch or listen if they wish.

INTRODUCTION

> If you don't lose weight, you will never see your daughter graduate!

These words are still chilling to this day. I was sitting in my doctor's office. My doctor had been taking care of me for the last ten+ years.

I was pre-diabetic, pre-hypertensive and found myself at 340 pounds. I had always been an athlete and am still now. I had never been this heavy. What happened?

Images of fat and skinny me

1999
340lbs & 46" waist

2014
195lbs & 32" waist

This is me at my heaviest:

This is me now:

HOW DID I LET THIS HAPPEN?

Why hadn't my friends said anything to me? 340 pounds!! WTH? I had always had a 32-inch waist, and now I am a 46-inch waist. What have I done?

This is crazy. How did I get used to this weight? This can't be right, 340 pounds! My daughter was just born, and I am experiencing a love that I never thought was possible. But now, there's a possibility that I won't see my own beautiful daughter graduate, and it's my fault!? What have I done?

I knew I was getting a little large, sure, with all the work. I definitely drink a lot of soda. Big box store soda is only five (5) cents a can when you break it down by case. Sure, there was some late-night pizza and Chinese food, but still 340 pounds? "Doc, this can't be right. Let's weigh me again."

The doctor holds her hand out with thumb and forefinger parallel to each other, saying:

"You are this close to getting diabetes!"

"You must be put on cholesterol-reducing and other serious medications right away!"

Now I must take pills? I have never had to do *that* before! What have I done? Who can I blame for this?

Looking back now and seeing the pictures, it's like looking at another person. I was 340 pounds, –that's 150 percent larger than I should be. What was happening? How did I let go of control over my own body? And better yet, how could I have put other priorities ahead of my own personal well-being?

As I drove directly from that doctor's appointment to the pharmacy to purchase the prescription pills, I looked at myself in the rearview mirror and realized, "My face is so pudgy. My belly is huge!"

Then later at dinner, while sitting at the table with my family, still thinking, "What have I done? As the breadwinner and head of the house, how could I have done this to myself? I've let myself and my family down. Something has got to change."

I have always been an athlete, a fighter, a competitor. I was a hustler, scrambling to be the winner at almost any cost. I played organized soccer, plenty of baseball, kickball, football, and even tennis. And now I am a 340-pound overweight POS? Woah!

I still remember the day that changed my life forever. The day I heard the most shocking and terrifying words from my doctor.

"If you don't lose weight, you will never see your daughter graduate!"

These words still haunt me to this day. They were like a cold slap in the face that woke me up from a deep sleep. A sleep that had lasted for years and had made me oblivious to the damage I was doing to myself.

Somewhere along the way, things changed. I stopped working out regularly. I started eating junk food more often. I drank soda like water. I ordered pizza or Chinese food late at night. I skipped breakfast and lunch and binged on dinner.

I knew these habits were bad for me, but I didn't care enough to change them. Or maybe I was in denial about how much they were affecting me. I didn't notice how much weight I was gaining over time. Or maybe I didn't want to notice. My clothes got tighter and tighter until they didn't fit anymore. But instead of losing weight to fit into my clothes, I bought bigger ones.

My friends and family saw how big I was getting, but they didn't say anything to me. Maybe they were afraid to hurt my feelings or start an argument. Maybe they thought it was none of their business or that it was just a phase. But it wasn't just a phase. It was a serious problem that was putting my life at risk.

I had developed pre-diabetes and pre-hypertension—two conditions that could lead to heart disease, stroke, kidney failure, blindness, amputation, or death if left untreated. And yet, even with these warning signs, I still didn't take action to improve my health until that day in the doctor's office when he told me those words that hit me like a ton of bricks:

"If you don't lose weight, you will never see your daughter graduate!"

INTRODUCTION

EVIL INSIDE

To this day, there are times when I feel the 340-pound person inside of me trying to get out. I need to actively fight back. I will not gain that weight back again! Today I intermittently fast, take supplements, and exercise often. It's no secret how to lose weight.

There are three pillars of health:

1. Diet
2. Exercise
3. Sleep

Others may add:

1. Morning sunlight
2. Surrounding oneself with positive people
3. Drinking a lot of water
4. Supplements

I agree with these additions, but my essentials still ring true. When people hear my story of weight loss, the very first thing they ask is, and I see it on their faces, "How did you do it?" It's as if there is some secret way to lose 130 pounds that no one knows about. It takes hard work, focus, redirection, change of lifestyle—which can all be summarized in one word:

Discipline!

Even now, there are moments when I feel like the person who weighed 340 pounds is trying to come back out. I must actively resist him. It's not a secret how to lose weight or how to keep it off—It's all about Discipline.

CHAPTER 1

LIFE DISCIPLINES

~~~

B ased on our conversations and experience, we divide life's objectives into four quadrants or domains.

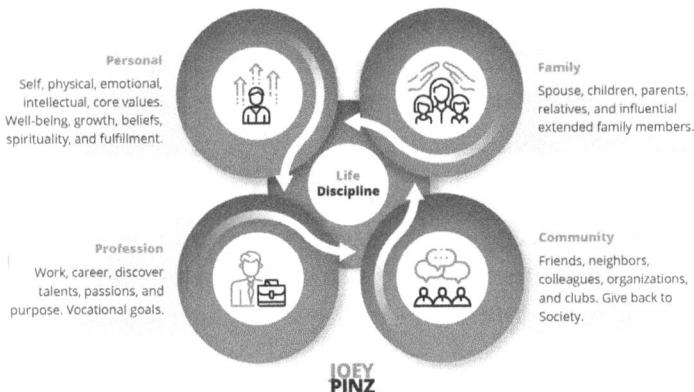

Life is a complex and diverse journey, encompassing multiple aspects. We can categorize our lives into four distinct Disciplines or areas that correspond to our roles, responsibilities, and interests: Personal, Family, Professional, and Community. Each discipline presents Discipline challenges and opportunities, and they can often intertwine, influence, and affect one another in diverse ways.

1. Personal Discipline: This Discipline is our individual identity, values, goals, health, and well-being. It includes our person-

ality, hobbies, spirituality, self-esteem, and self-care. Personal discipline is mega important because it shapes our sense of who we are and what we want in life.

2. Family Discipline: This Discipline shows how strongly we build our relationships with our partners, relatives, and children. It includes communication, intimacy, support, and conflict resolution. Family discipline is important; it provides us with love, belonging, and security.

3. Professional Discipline: This Discipline is our work or career path. It includes aspects such as our education, skills, income, and satisfaction. Professional discipline is important as it gives us a sense of purpose, achievement, and contribution.

4. Community Discipline: This Discipline is our involvement with society. It includes our social network, civic engagement, volunteering, and activism. Community discipline is important as it connects us with others who share our values and interests. We also include religion attendance and participlation to the Community Discipline.

These four Disciplines are not mutually exclusive or fixed; they can overlap or change over time depending on our circumstances and choices. A balanced life is one that integrates these Disciplines that meet our needs and aspirations in every area of our life.

PERSONAL

Personal
Self, physical, emotional, intellectual, core values. Well-being, growth, beliefs, spirituality, and fulfillment.

The personal areas are the domains of the Self: physical, emotional, and intellectual, well-being. Foundationally it includes beliefs, spirituality, and core values. It also focuses on one's own well-being, growth, and fulfillment. Discover your unique design, talents, heart, and thinking. Align your personal goals with your life's mission. Personal life Discipline refers to one's private life outside work and professional obligations. It encompasses various aspects such as health, well-being, hobbies, and leisure activities.

A healthy and fulfilling personal life is essential for overall well-being and happiness. Maintaining physical and mental health through exercise, healthy eating habits, and self-care activities can also contribute to a positive personal life. Engaging in hobbies and leisure activities, such as reading, playing sports, or acquiring new skills, brings about a sense of joy and fulfillment that extends beyond the boundaries of work. These activities can also help individuals manage stress and improve their mental health.

However, balancing personal life and professional life can be challenging. Long work hours, demanding deadlines, and other work-related stressors can interfere with personal life and relationships. Establishing clear boundaries and prioritizing personal time is crucial to maintain a healthy work-life balance.

In addition, individuals should also be mindful of their personal goals and values when making decisions about their personal life. Having a clear sense of personal values and priorities can help individuals make decisions that align with their goals and contribute to their happiness and well-being. Overall, the personal life domain is vital to an individual's well-being and should be nurtured and prioritized.

FAMILY LIFE DISCIPLINE

The family focuses on relationships with spouses, children, parents, relatives, and influential extended family members. It helps understand family history, dynamics, and values. It also helps align family goals with a life mission. Family life Discipline refers to an individual's experiences and relationships within their family unit. This Discipline various aspects such as communication, support, conflict resolution, and family traditions.

Family

Spouse, children, parents, relatives, and influential extended family members.

Family is often considered the most critical aspect of an individual's life. A strong and supportive family unit can provide a sense of belonging, comfort, and security. Positive family relationships can also contribute to an individual's emotional and mental well-being, self-esteem, and happiness.

ESSENTIAL COMPONENTS OF A HEALTHY FAMILY LIFE.

Communication allows family members to express their feelings, concerns, and needs, leading to better understanding and stronger relationships.

Supportive family relationships also involve a willingness to listen and show empathy towards each other.

Conflict resolution is another critical aspect of family life. Disagreements and conflicts are a normal part of family life. Still, the way they are resolved can significantly impact family relationships. Effective conflict resolution strategies, such as active listening and compromise, can help family members resolve conflicts while maintaining positive relationships.

Family *traditions* also play a vital role in the family life domain. Traditions, like celebrating holidays or participating in shared hobbies, can strengthen family bonds and create lasting memories.

Family life Discipline is a crucial aspect of an individual's life. Positive family relationships, effective communication, conflict resolution, and family traditions can contribute to an individual's well-being and happiness. It is essential to prioritize and nurture family relationships while recognizing and addressing any challenges that arise.

Family Life -Italy, 1978

It was the first day of the summer of 1978 and I had just completed third grade. My Italian immigrant father gave me a suitcase and asked me to put some clothes in it. He took me to the bus station in New Haven, CT, and instructed the bus driver to drop me off at terminal 1 at JFK airport in Queens, NYC. Before saying goodbye, he gave me a few items: a picture of my grandmother and uncle, my passport, $100, and a heartfelt kiss.

He instructed me as follows: When I landed in Italy, I was to find my grandmother and uncle at the airport. I was ten years old and I was highly excited as I boarded the bus for the 1.5-hour journey to JFK Airport. I was thrilled about traveling by plane across the ocean to my grandmother and uncle whom I had never visited or seen before. I could think of nothing else.

Can you imagine this scenario today? My father would have been arrested in today's world! But it was different then. The airline staff was very friendly and, when we landed, they ensured that I found my relatives. I spent ten weeks with them. That summer was the beginning of a tradition that would see me visiting them during many summers that followed.

Initially, I did not know any Italian or know any of my relatives. But, over the summer, I immersed myself in their culture. I played soccer with my cousins and impressed them with my skills, went to concerts and museums, played cards, and indulged in delicious food and occasional sips of wine. The abundance of food and activities was almost overwhelming at times. Family members would get into friendly arguments about who had the honor of feeding me. Each activity, interaction, and event allowed me to learn a little more Italian, understand my family better, and gain insights into Italian culture.

I became known as "filio di Paoluccio" (Paul's son). My last name means 'big bread' and my nickname among my friends was 'Joi' (Joey) short for 'Giuseppe.' So, I was "Joey, Paul's son." My Uncle Franco, a wonderful man, would always have me over and impart his experiences. His wife had died years before. I would have meals there, and a placemat was set up where my Aunt Amelia would sit when alive.

Anthony, another one of my uncles, moved to the States. Uncle Tony would tell me stories about how he hid my father and others in the woods to hide from the troops. Some bullet holes from that time were still visible on the village walls.

My family practically invented "farm to table." Money was not always necessary since many of the families would barter food and animal products. Eggs would be stored in cupboards because they did not need refrigeration because they were so fresh.

My father's home village was near Caserta, which is in the south near Naples. Rocoromano is a beautiful small village, where most of the inhabitants, at that time, were related to me somehow. During my visit, I had the opportunity to visit the stunning Amalfi coast and fell in love with it. It remains one of my favorite places in the world.

At a young age, I learned that the work ethic is very different in southern Italy. Let me share a story about my two cousins, Antonio and Franco. (I know what you are thinking, Italian cousins named Tony and Frank, no way… well, it's true.) They worked for the village, dealing with cleaning the streets or something similar. One Monday morning, when it was raining, I noticed they were not working, and I asked why. Their response was, "We don't work when it rains." I found it amusing and spent the day playing cards, drinking wine, and talking about girls with cousins Tony and Frank.

On Tuesday it was still raining, and they were still not working.

Wednesday was a beautiful clear day, and they still were not working. So, I asked, "Why are you not working?"

"You never start the week on a Wednesday," they answered.

I also learned that in Southern Italy, unlike the States, it's a bit improper to ask what someone does for a living. From that, one may discern the salary and the discussion of money is highly improper. Southern Italians generally do not connect themselves to their job. They simply work to live, not live to work, which differs from most of us in the West.

I learned at a young age how other cultures live differently than we work just as well. The lesson is that just because it's different, it doesn't mean it's better or worse. It's just different. And that's an example of tradition.

I thrived in the Italian environment. The family would engage in friendly arguments about who had the honor of feeding me. That's an example of resolving conflict in a healthy manner. Watching my family life – the conflict, the resolution of conflict, the tradition and the way they communicate helped build the essential components of Family Discipline.

I adore the Italians and appreciate their viewpoint. After all, I am Italian American. I still love Italy today and it has a special place in my heart.

In early childhood, I faced the formidable challenge of adapting to an entirely new country, complete with its own language and cultural norms. This transition required not just learning a new language but also assimilating into a host of unfamiliar customs and traditions. The prevailing philosophy around work and life in this new setting was markedly different from what I had known, demanding a profound shift in my perspective.

Navigating these complexities necessitated a significant degree of discipline. This discipline allowed me to make pivotal adjustments in various aspects of my life, ranging from the linguistic to the social and even the philosophical. By leveraging the power of discipline, I was able to bridge the cultural gap, adapt to my new surroundings, and assimilate the values and norms that were initially foreign to me. Thus, discipline served as a critical tool in facilitating my successful adaptation to a new cultural landscape.

PROFESSIONAL

Profession

Work, career, discover talents, passions, and purpose. Vocational goals.

Professional Life Discipline encompasses the realm of work, career, and calling. It involves exploring talents, passions, and purpose while aligning your vocational goals with your life mission. This Discipline around work's impact on a sense of purpose and fulfillment, encompassing elements like job satisfaction, career goals, and professional growth.

Job satisfaction is a crucial aspect of Professional Life Discipline, as it plays a significant role in one's life and identity. A fulfilling profession brings purpose, satisfaction, and a sense of accomplishment. It also contributes to financial stability and overall well-being. A job that aligns with personal values and interests can provide a unique fulfillment and purpose that other jobs may lack. Additionally, positive work relationships and a supportive work environment may also contribute to job fulfillment and satisfaction.

Career goals are another important aspect of professional life Discipline, offering direction and motivation in one's work. They contribute to a sense of accomplishment and career advancement. However, achieving a balance between professional and personal life can be challenging. The demands of long work hours, stress, and other work-related demands can interfere with personal life and strain family relationships. It is vital to establish clear boundaries and prioritize personal time to maintain a healthy work-life balance.

Overall, professional life Discipline is a vital aspect of an individual's overall well-being and should be given importance alongside personal and family obligations. It encompasses, all of which contribute to a rewarding and fulfilling vocation.

COMMUNITY

Community

Friends, neighbors, colleagues, organizations, and clubs. Give back to Society.

Community Discipline encompasses various essential areas of life, such as friends, neighbors, colleagues, organizations, and clubs. It involves giving back to society and building relationships based on shared beliefs. Being actively involved in the local community is a vital aspect of this Discipline.

Engaging in community life provides a sense of belonging, purpose, and fulfillment. Participation in social groups and community events allows individuals to connect with others and build meaningful relationships. Additionally, civic engagement and volunteering contribute to a sense of purpose and achievement while making a positive impact on the community.

Moreover, involvement in the community has significant benefits for mental and physical health. Social support and connections play a crucial role for overall well-being, and volunteering has been associated with lower rates of depression and improved mental health. However, participating in the community can present challenges like conflicts or limited resources. In these circumstances, effective communication, collaboration, and problem-solving are crucial. Social networks, community events, volunteering, and civic engagement are essential to community involvement. It is essential to prioritize and nurture community relationships within the community while acknowledging and tackling any challenges that arise.

SUMMARY

Life Disciplines encompasses various aspects and experiences that shape our lives as we grow and mature. They help us to reflect on our current realities while envisioning the desired life experiences that lead to fulfillment. The four Life Discipline personal, family, professional, and community hold unique significance and pose their own challenges. Furthermore, they can influence each other positively or negatively.

Each Discipline has its own importance and challenges, and they can influence each other positively or negatively. Moreover, these Disciplines are interconnected, meaning that positive or negative influences in one area can affect the others. By understanding and nurturing each life Discipline, we can strive for a more balanced and enriched life overall.

Discipline

By recognizing and nurturing these life Disciplines, we can navigate the different areas of our lives with intentionality and fulfillment.

CHAPTER 2
DISCIPLINE IS A SPECTRUM

> *"The only way that you can grow is to embrace the suck, to realize that the pain that you're feeling, the adversity that you're facing, it's not something that should discourage you, it's something that you should welcome into your life because it's the only way that you're going to grow stronger. Embrace the Discipline, embrace the suffering."*
> —David Goggins

David Goggins, a notable figure when it comes to Discipline, has a unique and captivating perspective on the subject. His book "*Can't Hurt Me*" is highly recommended for those interested in exploring Discipline.

Discipline has been a driving force behind my numerous achievements, such as losing over one hundred and thirty pounds and successfully running my company for over thirty years. I have had the opportunity to interview countless individuals on my podcast, asking them how Discipline's role in their lives, and their responses have been diverse and enlightening.

Our team's research has led us to view Discipline as a spectrum, with a range of approaches, techniques, and levels of intensities. Please note that this perspective is based solely on anecdotal evidence from our internal research and conversations on the Joey Pinz Discipline podcast. To comprehensively define the discipline spectrum, I have identified ten essential functions or characteristics.

These characteristics, presented in no particular order, include Focus, Restraint, Obedience, Mastery, Control, Routine, Order, Willpower, Direction, and Strictness. Through our extensive experience and countless interviews, we have found these ten characteristics to be comprehensive in depicting the various facets of Discipline.

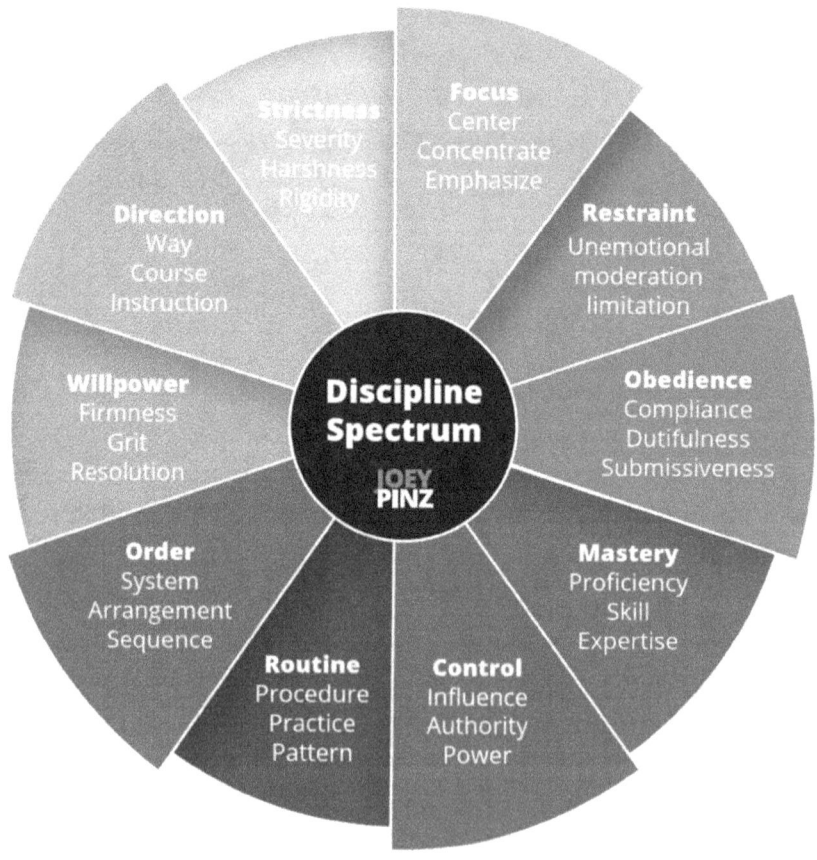

Discipline is often defined as the ability to follow rules, regulations, and commands. However, we believe that Discipline as a spectrum encompassing various aspects of traits related to self-regulation, goal setting, and skill development. Depending on the context and purpose, different levels and types of discipline may be desired. Here are some characteristics that can describe discipline as a spectrum: Discipline.

- **Focus**: The ability to concentrate on a specific task or objective without distractions, allowing for more efficient and effective goal achievement.
- **Restraint**: Resisting impulses, temptations, and distractions that could hinder progress towards our goals or go against our values, enabling us to avoid harmful or unnecessary actions and consequences.
- **Obedience**: Compliance with rules, regulations, and commands from authorities or institutions, promoting order, harmony, and safety in society.
- **Mastery**: The acquisition and application of knowledge, skills, and talents at a high-performance level within a particular field or domain, leading to improved conduct, competence, and confidence.
- **Control**: Managing our emotions, thoughts, and behaviors in various situations, enhancing our ability to cope with stress, challenges, and conflicts.
- **Routine**: Establishing and following regular activities or habits that support our goals or well-being, creating structure, stability, and consistency in our lives.
- **Order**: Organizing our environment, resources, and time in a logical and efficient manner, reducing clutter, waste, and chaos.
- **Willpower**: Persisting in pursuing our goals despite difficulties, obstacles, or setbacks, enabling us to overcome challenges, adversity, and failure.

- **Direction**: Setting clear, realistic goals aligned with our values and vision, helping us plan actions, measure progress, and evaluate outcomes.
- **Strictness**: Imposing the highest standards of quality, accuracy, and excellence on us or others, leading to optimal results, immense satisfaction, and distinguished recognition.

These characteristics are not mutually exclusive or fixed; they can vary in degree, intensity, and scope depending on the situation or person. A balanced approach to Discipline involves adapting these characteristics to our specific needs and preferences in order to gain optimal results.

Remember that self-Discipline is the foundation of Discipline begins with yourself.

THE ROLE OF DISCIPLINE

Discipline plays a crucial role in our lives, encompassing characteristics that contribute to our personal and social development. It promotes honesty, hard-working, motivation, and encouragement throughout life, fostering our goals and leading happy, successful lives.

> "The role of Discipline in life is to help us achieve our goals, transform our weaknesses into strengths, and cultivate the habits and mindset of success."
> —Robin Sharma

Discipling brings numerous benefits Some of the benefits of Discipline may be:

Developing healthy habits. It helps us to form positives that improve our health, productivity, and well-being. For example, by following a regular routine of exercise, diet, and sleep, we can grow our physical and mental fitness. Through self-control, we can avoid harmful temptations that could adversely impact ourselves or others.

Effective time management is another advantage of Discipline. It allows us to plan, set deadlines, allocate resources, and avoid distractions. This allows us to accomplish more in less time. By combatting procrastination, discipline fulfills our responsibilities promptly, reducing stress and increasing confidence and satisfaction.

Discipline also instills respect for ourselves and others. It teaches us to abide by societal rules, behave courteously, and consider the feelings of others with an open mind.

Furthermore, Discipline drives self-improvement. It motivates us to learn new skills, expand our knowledge, and continuously enhance ourselves. By setting high standards and accepting constructive feedback, we strive for personal growth and development.

Discipline helps us to face difficulties and overcome obstacles with courage and determination.

- We do not give up easily or lose hope when things go wrong.
- We learn from our mistakes and try again until we succeed.

Finally, Discipline helps us to deal with failures and setbacks with grace and resilience.

We do not let them affect our self-esteem or morale. We take them as learning opportunities and use them to improve ourselves.

- **Developing Healthy Habits**: Embracing Discipline helps us to form positive habits that improve our health, productivity, and overall well-being. For example, by following a regular routine of exercise, diet, and sleep, we can grow our physical and mental fitness. Additionally, by practicing self-control, we can avoid temptations that harm us or others.
- **Better Time Management**: Discipline helps us to manage our time effectively and efficiently. We learn to plan, set deadlines, allocate resources, and avoid distractions. This allows us to accomplish more in less time.

- **Overcoming Procrastination**: Discipline ensures we do not delay or avoid our responsibilities. We learn to prioritize our work and complete tasks on time. This reduces stress and anxiety and increases our confidence and satisfaction and allows us to accomplish more within shorter time frames.
- **Respect for Others**: Discipline teaches us to respect ourselves and others. It leads us to follow societal rules and regulations and behave politely and courteously with everyone. We also respect the opinions and feelings of others and listen to them with an open mind.
- **Self-improvement**: Discipline motivates us to learn new skills, acquire knowledge, and constantly improve. We set high standards for ourselves and strive to achieve them. We also accept constructive feedback from others and work on our weaknesses, propelling us toward personal development.
- **Overcoming Challenges**: Discipline helps us to face difficulties and overcome obstacles with courage and determination. We do not give up easily or lose hope when things go wrong. We learn from our mistakes and try again until we succeed.
- **Coping with Failures**: Discipline helps us to deal with failures and setbacks with grace and resilience. We do not let them affect our self-esteem or morale. We take them as learning opportunities and use them to improve ourselves.

WHAT DOES DISCIPLINE MEAN TO YOU?

When asking yourself the question, what is your response?

On the JPDC (Joey Pinz Discipline Podcast), I interview numerous guests about the role of Discipline in their lives. We carefully selected a sample set of results, which will be referred to in the book. For brief biographies of the guests, please consult the bibliography where their real names have been replaced with aliases. Here is a sample set of results.

JPDC GUEST: BATHSHEBA

As a personal branding expert, she uses Discipline to train herself and others to be consistent and congruent across different platforms and situations, both for herself and her clients. She also uses Discipline to follow a system of rules and expectations. Discipline helps her achieve her goals and build trust with her audience.

Through Disciplined practices, she stays on track with her objectives, allowing her to achieve her goals effectively. Moreover, Discipline plays a vital role in establishing trust with her audience, as it showcases her commitment to delivering on promises and maintaining authenticity in her branding efforts.

Her Disciplined approach not only strengthens her personal brand but also enables her clients to establish a strong and reliable brand identity. By employing Discipline in the realm of personal branding, she elevates her expertise and contributes to the success of those she serves.

JPDC GUEST: BETE

By expressing her personality and style through fashion, she believes in the power of Discipline. For her, dressing to impress is not just about looking good; it's also about feeling empowered, beautiful, confident, and sexy. Even when hitting the gym, she exhibits Discipline by consistently matching her workout outfits.

At work, she adheres to a Disciplined approach, opting for business attire over casual wear. This practice not only sets a professional tone but also influences her mood and mindset, preparing her to take on the day with determination and purpose. For her, Discipline in fashion is more than just a choice; it's a way of channeling her inner strength and projecting her best self to the world.

JPDC GUEST: ROCKSON

In dealing with his mental health issues and past trauma, he recognizes the importance of Discipline. For him, Discipline is needed to be curious about oneself, to ask meaningful questions, and to work with the answers.

He practices Discipline by seeking support from a therapist when needed and sharing his insights and experiences with others. This willingness to share and seek help contributes to his healing and personal growth.

Through the lens of Discipline, he navigates his journey towards emotional well-being and a deeper understanding of himself, ultimately leading to positive transformation and progress as an individual.

JPDC GUEST: ANTHONY

Discipline and objective in his discussion and acknowledging the world's diversity and complexity. Discipline helps him to bridge Discipline and positivity in America.

Assisting him to communicate his perspective and experience as a Muslim living in the United States, he emphasizes the importance of Discipline. He believes that Discipline is needed to open up the conversation between Muslims and non-Muslims, breaking down ignorance and misconceptions on both sides.

To achieve this, he practices Discipline by being respectful and objective in his discussions. He acknowledges the world's diversity and complexities within Islam and America.

Through Discipline, he effectively bridges the gap between Islam and America, striving to promote understanding, empathy, and harmony. His commitment to Disciplined communication plays a vital role in fostering connections and building bridges between different communities, leading to a more inclusive and empathetic society.

JPDC GUEST: SOPHIE

Sophie believes Discipline helps her be confident and empowered as a woman who speaks openly about her sexuality. She also values not letting other people's opinions or judgments affect her self-worth. Discipline stays true to herself and her vision and does not compromise on her integrity or authenticity.

She strongly advocates for confidence and empowerment as a woman who speaks openly about her sexuality. Importantly, she places great value on maintaining a strong self of self-worth, regardless of others' opinions or judgments.

Discipline plays a significant role in her life by allowing her to stay true to herself and her vision. It empowers her to uphold her integrity or authenticity without compromising on her values. Through Discipline, she navigates life with unwavering determination and stays true to herself, embracing her identity with pride and self-assurance.

JPDC GUEST: MICAH

He believes Discipline assists in the power of digital marketing and content creation for any business. He also values using free tools and building a following online. Discipline helps him to stay updated on the latest trends and strategies in his field and deliver quality results for his clients.

He believes in the power of digital marketing and content creation as essential elements for any business. He highly regards the utilization of free tools and the process of building a following online.

Discipline is the driving force behind his success, as it helps him stay updated and well-informed on the latest trends and strategies in the dynamic world of digital marketing. By constantly updating his knowledge and skill set, he consistently delivers high-quality results for his clients, effectively leveraging the power of digital platforms to propel the businesses forward.

JPDC GUEST: JOSEPHINE

She believes Discipline assists her in having a clear vision of where she wants to go and how to get there. She also values involving others in her journey and listening to their ideas. Discipline helps her stay focused on her goals and avoid distractions or detours.

She believes in having a clear vision of where she wants to go and how to get there. She places great importance on involving others in her journey and being receptive to their ideas and perspectives.

Discipline helps her stay focused on her goals and avoid distractions or detours that might hinder her progress. By adhering to a Disciplined mindset, she remains on track towards her objectives, while also fostering a collaborative and inclusive environment that values the input and contributions of others.

JPDC GUEST: GABRIEL

Gabriel believes that Discipline helps him overcome obstacles and achieve goals. He is a former professional basketball player who successfully used Discipline toughness, and personal initiative. His philosophy centers around the belief that hard work alone is insufficient for success, individuals must develop a personalized system and strategy that aligns with their goals.

As a former professional basketball player, he understands the power of Discipline to overcome challenges and achieve his goals. Now, he is a CEO and founder of a company that helps entrepreneurs and athletes develop their mindset, strategy, and accountability.

With numerous TEDx Talks under his belt, and over thirty books authored on Discipline, confidence, mental toughness, and personal initiative, he is a recognized authority in his field.

He believes that hard work is not enough to succeed. He emphasizes one needs to have a system and a strategy that works for them. By promoting a holistic approach, he aims to power individuals to thrive and achieve their full potential.

JPDC GUEST: VALENTINA

Valentia uses Discipline as a branch of knowledge. She is a nutritional therapist who helps people with health and wellness using nutritional science and lifestyle modifications. She needs Discipline as a branch of knowledge because she has to study and apply nutritional science to different cases and scenarios. She also needs to have Discipline of training because she has to follow specific guidelines and said nothing such as providing evidence-based advice and respecting client confidentiality. She may also need to discipline herself regarding eating habits, stress management, and mindset. As a nutritional therapist, she is dedicated to helping people with health and wellness using nutritional science and lifestyle modifications. Discipline plays a dual role.

Firstly, she needs Discipline as a branch of knowledge because she has to study and apply nutritional science to different cases and scenarios. This expertise enables her to tailor personalized solutions for her client's unique needs.

Secondly, she also needs to have Discipline as a practice of training. This involves following specific guidelines and standards in her profession, such as providing evidence-based advice and respecting client confidentiality.

Additionally, Discipline comes into play when guiding her clients on various aspects, including healthy eating habits, stress management, and cultivating a positive mindset. Both she and her clients benefit from Disciplined practices to foster positive, sustainable changes in their lives.

JPDC GUEST: OLIVER

Oliver also believes that Discipline is a branch of knowledge. He is a wealth advisor who helps people with investing and financial planning. He needs Discipline of knowledge of receiving of knowledge because he has to be familiar with different aspects of finance and economics. He also needs to have discipline as a wealth manager because he has to follow specific rules and regulations in his profession, such as being a fiduciary and disclosing any conflicts of interest. He may also need to discipline himself or his clients of managing their money and spending habits. As a wealth advisor he helps people with investing and financial planning. Discipline is essential in two key aspects of Discipline as a profession.

Firstly, he needs Discipline as a branch of knowledge because he has to be familiar with different aspects of finance and economics. This expertise allows him to provide informed and tailored advice to his clients.

Secondly, he also needs to have Discipline as a practice of training. To uphold the highest ethical standards, he must adhere to specific rules, and regulations in his profession, such as being a fiduciary and disclosing any conflicts of interest.

Finally, Discipline comes into play when guiding both himself or his clients in terms of managing their money and spending habits. By fostering financial practices, he helps his clients achieve their financial goals and secure a stable financial future.

JPDC GUEST: SAVANNAH

Savannah uses Discipline to help her to cope with bullying and racial discrimination. She has self—Discipline to do things in a controlled and habitual way, such as working as an executive in a downtown store. She also has the discipline to obey the level of behavior that she sets for herself or follows from others, such as handling demanding customers with professionalism and respect. Discipline helps her to grow and overcome challenges.

She finds Discipline to be a powerful tool in helping her to cope with bullying and racial discrimination. By cultivating a Disciplined approach, she developed the ability to handle situations in a controlled and habitual manner, such as working as an executive in a downtown store.

Furthermore, Discipline empowers her to adhere to rules or a code of behavior that she sets for herself or follows from others. This is particularly evident in how she handles demanding customers with professionalism and respect.

With Discipline as her ally, she has grown a thick skin, enabling her to confront challenges head-on and overcome diversity. This inner strength and resilience allow her to navigate difficult situations with grace and determination. Discipline serves as a pillar of support in her journey towards personal growth and triumph over difficult circumstances.

JPDC GUEST: AUTUMN

Autumn uses Discipline to train herself to do things in a controlled and habitual way. She has the Discipline tasks such as raising her kids, running her businesses, and building her email funnels. She also has the discipline to obey the high-level behavior that she sets for herself or follows from others. Discipline helps her to achieve and improve her performance.

With her unwavering Discipline, she trains herself to do things in a controlled and habitual way. Whether it's raising her kids, running her businesses, or building email funnels, she handles each responsibility with focused determination.

Additionally, she is committed to following her self-imposed rules and a code of behavior that she sets for herself or follows from others. This Disciplined approach helps her to achieve her goals and improve her performance.

Through Discipline, she effectively pursues her goals and continuously improves her performance in all aspects of her life. This resolute commitment to Discipline propels her forward, empowering her to achieve success and make steady progress in her endeavors.

JPDC GUEST: LEILANI

Leilani uses Discipline to help her overcome the challenges and traumas of her past, and to share her story with courage and clarity. She also uses therapy and writing to heal and empower herself and others who may feel alone or hopeless.

Leilani uses Discipline to assist her in conquering the challenges and traumas of her past; she bravely shares her story with courage and clarity. Utilizing therapy and writing to heal and empower herself, she embarks on a journey of healing and empowerment, not just for herself but also for others who may be struggling with feelings of isolation and hopelessness.

Through her courage and vulnerability, she creates a safe space for others to connect and find solace in knowing they are not alone. Her journey of healing serves as a beacon of hope, inspiring others to seek help and embark on their path towards recovery and empowerment.

JPDC GUEST: AUBREY

Aubrey uses Discipline to help her explore the connections between science, art, and nonverbal experiences in self-discovery and self-mastery. She also draws from her diverse background in academia, business management, philosophy, and coaching to understand how we work and how we know ourselves.

She uses Discipline for exploring the connections between science, art, and nonverbal experiences in self-discovery and self-mastery. Leveraging her diverse background in academia, business management, philosophy, and coaching, she delves into understanding the intricacies of human behavior and how we came to know ourselves.

By integrating these varied fields of expertise, she navigates the complexities of the human experience, seeking insights that enable individuals to better comprehend themselves and achieve self-mastery. Her interdisciplinary approach fosters a holistic and multifaceted understanding of the human psyche, providing valuable tools for personal growth and self-awareness.

JPDC GUEST: ANDRES

Andres uses Discipline to help him be a social entrepreneur who identifies and solves problems with a business perspective and a social impact. He also explains the difference between a social venture and a nonprofit organization regarding their objectives, profits, and donations.

He uses Discipline to become a social entrepreneur, who identifies and solves problems with a business perspective and a social impact. He also explains the difference between a social venture and a nonprofit organization regarding their objectives, profits, and donations.

By combining his business acumen with a passion for social change, he endeavors to create ventures that not only achieve financial success but also generate meaningful and sustainable benefits for the community. Furthermore, he shares insights into the unique characteristics of social ventures compared to traditional nonprofit organizations, shedding light on their distinct approaches to achieving their missions. Through his endeavors, he aims to foster a greater understanding of the possibilities and potentials in the realm of social entrepreneurship.

JPDC GUEST: AXTON

Axton uses Discipline in helping him to be an entrepreneur who is aggressively curious, hurdles obstacles, figures things out, focuses on solutions, and pushes for innovation. He also acknowledges that entrepreneurship requires hard work, planning, and perseverance in the face of ups and downs. With a determined spirit, he fearlessly tackles obstacles, seeking solutions and pushing the boundaries of innovation.

While pursuing entrepreneurship, he understands that success requires hard work, careful planning, and perseverance in the face of ups and downs.

His journey as an entrepreneur is fueled by relentless curiosity and an unyielding drive to overcome challenges. By fostering a solution-oriented approach and embracing innovation, he aspires to carve out a path of accomplishment and make a meaningful impact in the business world.

JPDC GUEST: BROOKLYN

Brooklyn uses Discipline to create and sell software as a service (SaaS) platform. She believes persistence is the key to success in any new business venture and requires understanding the customer and changing the perspective.

Brooklyn uses Discipline to be dedicated to creating and selling software as a service (SaaS) platform. According to her, persistence plays a vital role in success in any new business venture. To excel in this venture, she emphasizes the importance of understanding the customer and changing the perspective as needed.

With unwavering determination, she navigates the challenges that come with building and selling a SaaS platform. By placing a strong emphasis on customer needs and being open to continuous improvement, she aims to carve out a successful and sustainable path in the competitive world of software development and entrepreneurship.

JPDC GUEST: DIEGO

Diego uses Discipline to help start and grow his own small business, which requires a lot of freedom, innovation, and change. He also implies Discipline for improving families and communities through small businesses.

Diego uses Discipline as a method of helping him to start and grow his own small business, which requires a lot of freedom, innovation, and change. He also implies that Discipline is essential for improving families and communities through small businesses.

As he embarks on this entrepreneurial journey, he embraces the freedom that comes with owning a small business. Encouraging innovation and the willingness to adapt to changing circumstances, he navigates the challenges and opportunities that arise along the way.

He emphasizes the importance of Discipline as a driving force for success, not only in business but also in creating a positive impact on families and communities. Through Discipline practices and thoughtful decision-making, he strives to build a thriving small business that contributes to his local community and beyond.

JPDC GUEST: LELAND

Leland uses Discipline to overcome adversity. As a publicist, podcaster, speaker, author, blogger, and broadcaster who works in the sports and entertainment industry, he uses Discipline in adversity in all shapes and sizes, such as having two open-heart surgeries, two strokes, a motorcycle accident, and being hospitalized by Covid. He also uses discipline to provide humorous presentations that give takeaways to his audience and make them feel something. He believes that discipline can help anyone be a Disciplined version of themselves and achieve their goals.

As a multi-faceted professional working in the sports and entertainment industry, he wears various hats—publicist, podcaster, speaker, author, blogger, and broadcaster. Through his diverse career, he relies on Discipline to overcome adversity in all shapes and sizes, including enduring two open-heart surgeries, two strokes, a motorcycle accident, and being hospitalized by Covid.

Discipline serves as a powerful tool in his arsenal as he crafts presentations that are. both helpful and humorous, leaving a lasting impact on his audience. His talks offer valuable takeaways while evoking emotional responses, leaving attendees feeling moved and inspired.

With a deep-rooted belief in the transformative power of Discipline, he is a firm advocate that anyone can harness this quality to become the best version of themselves and achieve their goals. Through his own experiences and achievements, he exemplifies the profound impact Discipline can have on personal growth and success.

JPDC GUEST: RUBY

Ruby uses Discipline to cope with life. As an author, speaker, and mother who inspires and empowers people to overcome their own tribulations and find hope and healing in various areas of life, she uses Discipline with her lifelong disability of legal blindness, divorce, and the death/loss of her beloved husband at thirty-eight. She also uses discipline to write heartfelt meditations on her passions related to her life experiences, such as her disability, faith, motherhood, grief and loss, solo parenting, and empowerment. She believes that discipline can help anyone to thrive in all things.

As an author, speaker, and mother she inspires and empowers people to overcome their own tribulations and find hope and healing in various areas of life. In facing her own tribulations, including her lifelong disability of legal blindness, divorce, and the heartbreaking loss of her beloved husband at thirty-eight, she turns to Discipline as a guiding force.

Discipline enables her to navigate the complexities of her life experiences and channel them into heartfelt meditations on her passions. Through her writing, she explores topics such as her disability, faith, motherhood, grief and loss, solo parenting, and empowerment.

Her firm belief is that Discipline can help anyone transform from enduring immense tribulations to thriving in all aspects of life. By demonstrating resilience and strength in the face of adversity, she exemplifies how Discipline can be harnessed to triumph over life's challenges and emerge stronger and more empowered.

JPDC GUEST: ODIN

Odin uses Discipline to pursue his goals and passions. As a CEO, entrepreneur, and speaker who has overcome challenges and achieved success in his personal and professional life, he uses his goals and passions, such as running, tennis, skiing, and legal education. He also uses discipline to learn Discipline and improve himself, such as hiring a coach to help him tell stories for his TEDx talk. He believes discipline can help anyone break their fears and live a fulfilling life.

As a CEO, entrepreneur, and speaker who has overcome challenges and achieved success in his personal and professional life. The driving force behind his accomplishments is Discipline, which he applies diligently to pursue his goals and passions.

From pursuits like running, tennis, skiing, to expanding his legal knowledge, Discipline is what fuels his drive to excel in various aspects of life. Whether it's honing existing skills or acquiring new ones, he embraces Discipline as a means to continuously improve and grow.

A testament to his belief in the power of Discipline, he hired a coach to refine his storytelling abilities for TEDx talk. This example underscores how Discipline propels him to confront his fears and embrace opportunities for personal development.

His conviction is that Discipline can help anyone overcome their fears and live a fulfilling life. Through his journey, he serves as an inspiring example of how Discipline can be harnessed to unlock one's potential and achieve greatness in all spheres of life.

JPDC GUEST: AALIYAH

Aaliyah uses Discipline to listen for emotional reasons. As a master mediator, negotiator, and author who has resolved many cases involving human conflict and complex problems. She uses Discipline deeply to what people are saying and not saying, how they say it, and what they feel.

As an accomplished master mediator, negotiator, and author who has resolved many cases involving human conflict and complex problems, she attributes her success to Discipline.

Discipline guides her approach to listen deeply to what people are saying and not saying, how they say it, and what they feel. By honing this Disciplined approach, she gains valuable insights into the core of conflicts and the underlying dynamics at play.

Moreover, Discipline enables her to manage her own emotions and reactions effectively, ensuring that she remains composed and focused even in challenging situations. This self-Discipline contributes to her ability to create synergy among individuals with diverse personalities and interests.

Her belief is that most conflict starts with tension, which can be diffused through holding a sense of calm and composure. This kind of equanimity is nurtured by Discipline, enabling her to deftly navigate through complex disputes and facilitate resolutions that bring about positive change and harmony.

JPDC GUEST: GERALT

Geralt loves Discipline helping him achieve his goals, follow his passion, and cope with challenges. He has worked in tech for 45 years despite facing discrimination and unfairness. He also mentions that fairness is what you make of it, which shows his Discipline in having a positive attitude and not giving up.

Discipline can also be understood as a specific branch of knowledge, learning, or practice. In this sense, he has Discipline in the technology field, which he has been involved with for a long time. He probably has a lot of expertise and skills acquired through systematic training and education.

With a strong emphasis on Discipline, he offers guidance in attaining goals, pursuing passions, and overcoming obstacles. Despite encountering discrimination and unfairness, he has devoted forty-five years to working in the tech industry, showcasing remarkable perseverance.

His perspective on fairness reflects his Disciplined approach to maintaining a positive attitude and refusing to succumb to adversity. He understands that one's outlook on fairness is a matter of personal choice and demonstrates resilience through challenging circumstances.

Moreover, Discipline in this context, can be viewed as a specialized branch of knowledge, learning, and practice. In this sense, having been immersed in the technology field for an extended period, he likely possesses extensive expertise and skills acquired through systematic training and education.

His commitment to Discipline has played a pivotal role in his enduring career and continues to empower him to face challenges head-on while maintaining a forward-looking mindset. By embodying Discipline in his approach to work and life, he is an inspiring example of how dedication and positivity can pave the way for long-term success and personal fulfillment.

JPDC GUEST: AUDREY

Audrey uses Discipline for planning and research, learning self-control, obedience, and respect for different cultures, traveling more, and learning another language. She also mentions that preparing before traveling is essential, which shows her Discipline in patience and researching.

Audrey exemplifies Discipline in various aspects of her life. She utilizes it for planning and research, enabling her to approach tasks and endeavors with a well-prepared mindset. Discipline helps her to cultivate self-control, obedience, and respect, especially when engaging with different cultures during her travels. Moreover, she channels her Disciplined approach into her passion for exploring new places and learning foreign languages.

By prioritizing preparation before her journeys, she showcases her commitment to Discipline in planning and researching. This Disciplined approach not only enriches her travel experiences but also fosters a deeper understanding and appreciation of the diverse cultures she encounters. Audrey's dedication to Discipline serves as a valuable lesson in how structured and purposeful actions can lead to more fulfilling and enriching life experiences.

JPDC GUEST: HUNTER

Hunter uses Discipline as a way of learning and behaving. Helping them learn about the effects of stretching on their muscles and how to avoid injury. Practice of training people to obey rules or a code of behavior, using punishment to correct disobedience" or "a branch of knowledge, typically studied in higher education." In this context, a human might say that discipline is a way of operating and behaving.

Hunter embraces Discipline as a fundamental approach to both learning and behavior. His focus lies in helping others understand the impact of stretching on muscles and how to prevent injuries effectively.

In the context of his work, Discipline is viewed as a practice of training individuals to adhere to specific rules and codes of conduct. By instilling Discipline, they aim to promote obedience and correct any tendencies towards disobedience through appropriate measures.

Moreover, Discipline is perceived as a branch of knowledge, often studied in higher education. Within this framework, Hunter considers Discipline as a way of learning and behaving. This Disciplined approach to education and behavior ensures a structured and purposeful path towards understanding and implementing essential principles related to stretching, muscle health, and injury prevention. Through their Disciplined guidance, they empower others to adopt healthy habits and optimize their physical well-being.

JPDC GUEST: CLAIRE

Claire uses Discipline to pursue her passion and goals with dedication and perseverance. She is growing and improving her skills as a soccer player and an entrepreneur. She is also Disciplined in adapting challenges and opportunities that come with starting a business. Discipline enables her to be Disciplined and motivated.

Discipline plays a role in their life by helping them to pursue their passion and goals with dedication and perseverance. They are Disciplined in training and improving their skills as a soccer player and an entrepreneur. When adapting to new challenges and opportunities that come with starting a business, they approach them with Discipline and adaptability, which enables them to be resilient and motivated.

Their Disciplined approach fosters resilience and motivation, allowing them to navigate through setbacks and keep moving forward toward their objectives. By embodying Discipline in both their athletic and entrepreneurial pursuits, they exemplify how this quality can lead to success and personal growth in various aspects of life.

JPDC GUEST: WESTON

Weston uses Discipline to plan and anticipate the potential risks and challenges that their business might face. They are disciplined dispensing legal advice and guidance that is tailored to the specific needs and goals of their clients. They are also disciplined in creating Discipline resources and tools to help other business owners protect their assets and interests. Discipline enables them to be real and trustworthy.

Discipline plays a role in their life by helping them to plan ahead and anticipate the potential risks and challenges that their business might face. As legal advisors, they exhibit Discipline by offering and guidance that is tailored to the specific needs and goals of their clients.

Furthermore, they are also Disciplined in creating valuable resources and tools to help other business owners protect their assets and interests. Their Disciplined approach ensures that these resources are comprehensive, practical, and reliable.

Through their commitment to Discipline, they cultivate a professional and trustworthy reputation. By adhering to Disciplined practices, they build credibility and foster strong relationships with their clients and peers in the business community. Discipline serves as the cornerstone of their success, guiding them to be proactive, reliable, and highly effective in their legal counsel and support for businesses.

JPDC GUEST: KINSLEY

Discipline plays a significant role in Kinsley's life. It helps them to cope with the unpleasant and challenging situations that they encounter in their personal and professional life. It also helps them to improve their skills and performance by learning from their mistakes and taking corrective actions. Discipline helps them to grow as a person and as a professional.

Discipline plays a significant role in their life. It helps them to cope with the unpleasant and challenging situations that they encounter in their personal and professional life. By adhering to Disciplined practices, they are equipped to effectively cope with adversity and overcome obstacles.

It also helps them to improve their skills and performance by learning from their mistakes and taking corrective actions. This dedication to Disciplined self-improvement enables them to enhance their skills and performance, paving the way for growth both as an individual and as a professional

Through Discipline, they cultivate resilience and a commitment to excellence, propelling them forward on their journey of personal and career development. The Disciplined approach they embrace becomes the foundation of their success, driving them to thrive in the face of challenges and continually reach new heights in their personal and professional pursuits.

JPDC GUEST: DELILAH

Discipline plays a role in Delilah's life by helping them to pursue their interests and passions. They are writing and reading books, learning new things, and creating content for their podcast. They are also disciplined in managing time and energy and choosing when and how to interact with others. Discipline allows them to be focused and self-reliant.

Discipline takes center stage in their life as it guides them to actively pursue their interests and passions. They display Discipline in various areas, such as maintaining a consistent reading habit, acquiring new knowledge, and crafting content for their podcast.

Furthermore, Discipline plays a crucial role in their time and energy management. They exhibit a Disciplined approach in determining when and how to engage with others, ensuring they allocate their resources efficiently and purposefully.

Through their commitment to Discipline, they foster a sense of independence and self-reliance. This Disciplined mindset empowers them to take charge of their pursuits, make informed decisions, and navigate through life with a strong sense of purpose and direction. By embracing Discipline in their daily endeavors, they cultivate a proactive and determined attitude that enables them to pursue their passions and interests with unwavering focus and dedication.

Are any of these responses like yours? Do you relate to any of the responses?

SPECTRUM

Let's dive deeper into the ten characteristics of the Joey Pinz Discipline spectrum.

1-FOCUS

> "Discipline, focus, and endurance are what it takes to be the greatest at this sport."
> —Jordan Burroughs

We view Focus in regard to Discipline as the ability to follow through with whatever you do and to make yourself do something necessary when you could be doing something more pleasant. It requires planning, setting goals, finding motivation, and surrounding yourself with people who practice self-discipline.

For Instance:

- Focus in discipline allows you to zero in on your most important tasks, even when distractions are abundant.
- By maintaining focus, you're better equipped to adhere to a predetermined plan, thereby turning your goals into reality.
- A disciplined focus helps you muster the willpower to choose necessary tasks over momentary pleasures, ensuring long-term success.

- Cultivating focus through discipline enhances your ability to find and maintain motivation, acting as the driving force behind your endeavors.
- Surrounding yourself with disciplined individuals can bolster your own focus, creating a mutually reinforcing environment conducive to achievement.

Synonyms include:

- Center
- Concentrate
- Emphasize
- Highlight
- Spotlight

Discipline and Focus go hand in hand when it comes to achieving success. Focus plays a vital role in Discipline can be broken down into three key elements: Center, Concentrate, and Emphasize.

Centering involves focusing on your core values and beliefs. By centering yourself, you can maintain a strong sense of purpose and stay motivated towards your goals. When you're centered, you're less likely to get sidetracked by distractions or obstacles that come your way. You have a clear understanding of what's important to you, and you're willing to do whatever it takes to achieve your goals.

Concentrating involves directing your attention toward a specific task or goal. It's easy to get distracted in today's world, with so many things vying for our attention. However, by concentrating your energy and focusing on what's essential, you can stay on track and make progress toward goals. When you concentrate, you're more likely to produce high-quality work and achieve success.

Emphasizing involves putting a strong emphasis on your goals and priorities. By placing a strong importance on what's important, you're more likely to achieve success and maintain Discipline. When you emphasize your goals, you're less likely to get sidetracked. You have a clear understanding of what you want to achieve, and you're willing to put in the work to make it happen.

Focus plays a crucial role in ***Discipline.*** Centering, concentrating, and emphasizing are three critical elements of Focus that can help you achieve success and maintain Discipline yourself, concentrating on what's essential, and emphasizing your goals, you can stay on track and achieve the success you desire. With discipline and focus, Discipline overcomes any obstacles that come your way and achieve your dreams.

When it comes to Discipline, we consider Focus as the ability to stay committed and determined in your actions, even when faced with more enjoyable alternatives. This requires planning, goal-setting, finding motivation, and surrounding yourself with individuals who embody self-discipline.

In essence, Focus within Discipline means channeling your efforts towards what truly matters, despite potential distractions or temptations. It involves staying on track with your objectives, making deliberate choices, and avoiding procrastination or giving in to immediate gratification.

To practice this, you need to set clear goals, create a roadmap to achieve them, and draw motivation from your aspirations. Surrounding yourself with like-minded individuals who exhibit self-discipline can provide valuable support and reinforcement on your journey towards success. With a disciplined focus, you can tackle challenges, make progress, and stay dedicated to your path of personal growth and achievement.

Challenge your perceptions and don't allow negative thoughts or limiting beliefs to hinder you from pursuing your goals.

Engage in motivational activities that inspire or bring happiness before tackling challenging tasks.

In essence, these practices encourage you to confront self-doubt and negative mindset patterns while finding sources of motivation and positivity to fuel your efforts. By challenging perceptions and embracing motivation, you can overcome mental barriers and approach tasks with a renewed sense of confidence and enthusiasm.

Associate comfort with failure; don't be too hard on yourself. Embrace mistakes as opportunities to learn and grow, and then move forward.

Meditation is a powerful practice that can enhance focus, reduce stress, and foster self-awareness.

To improve discipline, remove distractions and temptations from your surroundings. Create an environment that contrasts with distractions by intentionally eliminating sources of temptation.

In summary, these practices advocate for self-compassion and learning from failures, utilizing meditation for improved focus and self-awareness, and proactively creating an environment conducive to discipline and productivity.

HOW HAVE I USED FOCUS AS RELATED TO DISCIPLINE IN MY LIFE:

The journey through my "Technology and Business" experience offers a vivid example of how focus, as a component of discipline, can shape one's path and drive success. Much like the intricate processes of coding and game development, focus demands an unwavering attention to detail and a commitment to seeing tasks through to completion. My early fascination with technology, particularly with the BASIC programming language, was not just about the joy of discovery; it was a disciplined focus on a field that was burgeoning with possibilities.

This focus was further honed through my ventures with my friend Jerry in creating our game, 'Quest', for Bulletin Board Systems. The discipline to stay focused, even when faced with initial shortcomings, led to the eventual success of our software application. Additionally, my experience in high school, balancing an active social life with a deep engagement in computer courses, is a testament to the power of focus in maintaining balance and excelling in chosen areas of interest.

The eventual realization that a formal education was essential for my career progression underscores how focus in discipline is not just about the dedication to a single skill but also about understanding and adapting to the broader requirements of one's aspirations. This narrative illustrates how a focused approach, much like the detailed and meticulous nature of programming, is crucial in navigating the multifaceted journey towards personal and professional growth.

TECHNOLOGY AND BUSINESS

Ever since I was a pre-teen and received my first computer and Atari 500, I have been hooked on technology. I taught myself the BASIC (Beginners' all-purpose symbolic instruction code) computer language and dreamt of doing this as a career.

The power of BASIC was never to be underestimated, and this became a mantra among application developers and programmers. I quickly grasped the language and found immense joy in the freedom and flexibility it provided. Understanding computer languages allowed me to view technology from an inside perspective, where the solutions seemed limitless. I cherished this unique knowledge, as only a handful of people shared my understanding and appreciation for it, making it feel like a special and exclusive realm.

In this journey, I had found my true calling—a passion that would fuel my path forward. The allure of technology and programming had deeply captured my heart, and I knew that I had discovered something truly extraordinary.

As the eldest child of Italian and French-Canadian parents, I found myself at a crossroads.

My father, an Italian immigrant, worked as a welder and had various side hustles, including welding, construction, and general labor jobs. I was often recruited to assist him in these endeavors, where he imparted valuable life lessons.

He taught me how to interact with customers professionally, plan ahead for each job, and prioritize safety when setting up a job site. These lessons remain with me to this day, as I still take safety precautions, like tying a knot around something sturdy when laying an extension cord, to prevent accidents.

Furthermore, I was involved in creating quotes for customers and handling invoices, which gave me exposure to basic accounting principles. Although I learned valuable skills from working with my hands, I knew deep down that my future lay in a different direction.

I knew working with my hands was not the future for me. This would confuse my parents at first, but they would soon appreciate my passion. I loved technology and saw myself involved with it for the rest of my life.

One of the most defining aspects of technology is its constant state of change—a double-edged sword. Before the World Wide Web, bulletin board systems or BBSs were prevalent. These were individual computers running BBS platform software, limited to single-user access. Connected to a dedicated phone line via a modem, BBSs allowed only one user at a time. Attempting to connect while someone else was already using it would result in a busy signal. The functionalities were quite basic, limited to software trading and a rudimentary emailing system. Additionally, users could engage in live "games" while online. These were text-based games.

Zork holds the distinction of being the first-ever text-based game. I distinctly recall my first encounter with Zork:

Upon encountering a gate with no keyhole, knocker, or handle, I attempted various actions to open it. I tried hitting it with my sword, kicking it, throwing rocks at it, attempting to burn it with a torch, charging at it, and hitting it with a blunt mace—all to no avail. After hours of frustration, it finally dawned on me to try a different approach. I uttered the words, "Open Sesame."

To my surprise, the door obediently opened.

Such was the captivating and often perplexing nature of text-based games. The absence of graphics or visual cues challenged players to think creatively and use their imagination to navigate through virtual worlds. However, the thought of current-day multiplayer, multi-location, complete graphic engine, and multilingual Xbox games was inconceivable in those early days of gaming.

Amidst this fascination with the evolving world of gaming, we decided to embark on our own creative journey. My great friend Jerry and I set out to create a game for the Bulletin Board Systems. Our collaborative effort led to the development of a dungeon and dragons-type adventure game called Quest. While it was okay, we recognized that it fell short of greatness.

Back then, if people liked an application, they would voluntarily send money, and we set up a PO Box in our town to receive their letters of appreciation and checks. The response was overwhelming, and we received around $5,000 in 1980 money, making our first software application endeavor a great success.

In high school, despite having a very active social life and being involved in soccer, I found myself drawn to computer courses in our fortunate computer lab. I enjoyed the problem-solving aspect of programming, and the time would fly by when I was immersed in it. Though I also dabbled in building "white box" computers, it was the software that truly excited me.

As graduation approached, I eagerly sought computer programming jobs, confident in my programming skills. However, to my shock and dismay, I realized that nobody would hire me without a bachelor's degree, regardless of my programming expertise. This realization left me dumbfounded, prompting the decision to pursue a college education. I needed to go to college!

> "Discipline is the bridge between goals and accomplishment, and focus is the light that illuminates the path."
> —Steve Marabol

DISCIPLINE ELEMENT LESSON LEARNED: FOCUS
WHAT DOES FOCUS MEAN TO YOU?

When asking yourself the question, what is your response?

On the JPDC (Joey Pinz Discipline Podcast), I interviewed numerous guests about the role of "Focus." We carefully selected a sample set of results, which will be referred to in the book. For brief biographies of the guests, please consult the bibliography where their real names have been replaced with aliases. Here is a sample set of results. I *focused* on and determined my passion for technology. My guests focused on other things.

As we delve deeper into the stories of our esteemed podcast guests, the theme of focus emerges as a pivotal aspect of their disciplined approach to life and work. Each guest, in their unique journey, has demonstrated the profound impact of honing their focus to achieve remarkable accomplishments. Similar to how my own experiences with technology required a laser-like focus, these individuals have channeled their energies and attention to excel in their respective fields. From artists meticulously perfecting their craft to entrepreneurs strategically navigating the complexities of the business world, the disciplined application of focus has been a consistent driver of their success. These narratives not only underscore the importance of focus in discipline but also provide valuable insights into how concentrated efforts, guided by clear goals, can lead to extraordinary achievements and personal growth.

JPDC GUEST DIEGO

Diego views focus as an essential element in business. He mentions the importance of clearly understanding business goals, metrics, and values and aligning them with the priorities of different teams, such as sales, manufacturing, and technology. Diego emphasizes the need for virtual co-location, where everyone reads from the same book, to ensure everyone is on the same page.

He also suggests having a chief customer officer who owns the end-to-end process and focuses on the customer interactions, ensuring a customer-centric approach.

On a personal level, Diego follows certain practices to maintain focus. He prioritizes self-care by drinking water, eating fruits, and exercising regularly. He also spends quality time with his family. He believes having a balanced routine, which includes personal and business-related activities is instrumental in achieving success in all aspects of life.

JPDC GUEST AXTON

From Axton's perspective, an entrepreneur is aggressively curious and focused on solving problems. They push for innovation and are constantly striving to overcome obstacles. Axton emphasizes that being an entrepreneur is not just a title; it's a mindset characterized by a strong work ethic, consistency, and resilience in the face of uncertainties.

For Axton, planning and measurement are vital components of achieving success in entrepreneurship. He encourages entrepreneurs to stay focused and driven, navigating through the highs and lows that come with the journey. With determination and sharp focus, entrepreneurs can forge their paths towards accomplishing their goals.

JPDC GUEST ANDRES

Andres considers Focus to be crucial for achieving mastery and efficiency. By concentrating on his strengths, he can deliver superior results in a shorter time frame. He firmly believes in repeated practice to attain mastery and develop a game-changing skill when it truly counts. Additionally, Andres advocates for collaborating with experts in other domains to streamline his Focus on what he excels at and establish an efficient system.

His goal is to save time, energy, and resources by creating an exceptionally efficient system. Andres sees Focus as a means to gain a competitive edge through both efficiency and mastery. By homing in on his core competencies and optimizing his approach, he seeks to achieve excellence and stand out in his endeavors.

JPDC GUEST LEILANI

Leilani deeply appreciates the significance of Focus in her life. She recalls a crucial moment when she had to concentrate intensely on a red dot, which ultimately led her to achieve a specific goal: qualifying for nationals. This experience solidifies her belief in the essential role of focus in attaining success and reaching one's goals. It underscores the idea that maintaining focus is a vital ingredient for accomplishing significant milestones and realizing one's aspirations.

JPDC GUEST AUBREY

Aubrey considers Focus to be a dynamic process involving entering the "flow state," where she becomes fully engrossed in a task. She emphasizes the importance of occasionally taking breaks and stepping back to gain a fresh perspective. Referring to scientific studies, she highlights the benefits of short breaks during work, which can lead to improved productivity and creativity when returning to the task.

In Aubrey's view, science and art complement each other in helping us comprehend and narrate the story of our lives. Moreover, she firmly believes that physical fitness plays a significant role in mental health and overall well-being and should be incorporated into therapeutic practices.

For Aubrey, Focus is not just about deep concentration but also about finding harmony between mental and physical aspects to enhance one's life experience.

JPDC GUEST BATHSHEBA

Bathsheba views Focus as critical to achieving one's vision and leaving a legacy. She believes that Discipline is necessary to stay on the path toward one's vision and to avoid distractions or wasteful activities that may hinder progress. Bathsheba also implies that Focus is linked to maturity, wisdom, and patience, as it requires a level of clarity and dedication to pursue a specific goal. Overall, Bathsheba values Focus as a critical attribute in achieving success and making a meaningful impact.

JPDC GUEST ROCKSON

Rockson views Focus as essential for starting the day on the right foot. He believes that he can set himself up for a successful day by focusing on specific activities, such as cold plunges, journaling, meditation, and reading inspirational books. Rockson finds that focusing on these activities allows him to be more present, grounded, and mindful throughout the day, which ultimately helps him feel more in control and less rushed. Rockson also believes mindfulness and focus are crucial for personal growth and spiritual enlightenment.

2-RESTRAINT

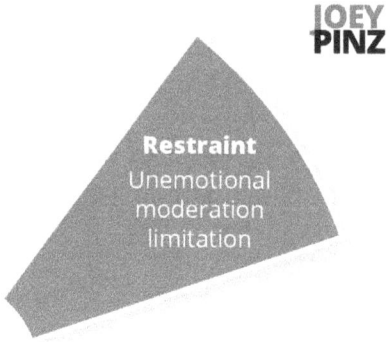

> *"Discipline and restraint are the foundation of a virtuous life; without them, we are easily swayed by our impulses and desires."*
> —Epictetus

Restraint is a measure or condition that keeps someone or something under control or within limits. The action of keeping someone or something under control is deprivation or restriction of personal liberty or freedom of movement.

For Instance:

- Restraint in discipline enables you to resist impulsive actions, allowing for thoughtful decision-making aligned with your goals.
- Employing restraint helps you manage emotional reactions, thereby facilitating rational choices in high-stress situations.
- Through disciplined restraint, you can avoid overindulgence in pleasurable activities that might derail your long-term objectives.
- Practicing restraint allows you to conserve resources, such as time and energy, focusing them on tasks that truly matter.

- Restraint serves as the gatekeeper of discipline, preventing you from veering off course and ensuring you stay committed to your established plans.

Other Synonyms are:
- Unemotional
- Moderation
- Limitation
- Dispassionate
- Understatement, especially of artistic expression

Restraint is an essential component of Discipline, which involves controlling one's impulses and desires. It is a crucial skill that can help us make rational decisions, avoid negative consequences, and succeed. Restraint can be broken down into three key elements: Unemotional, moderation, and limitation.

Unemotional restraint is the ability to control one's emotions and remain calm and rational in difficult situations. It is often said that emotions are the enemy of Discipline, which is true in many ways. Emotions can cloud our judgment and lead us to make impulsive decisions that may have negative consequences. By cultivating unemotional restraint, we can learn to control our emotions and make rational decisions that align with our goals.

Moderation restraint involves the ability to control one's desires and avoid excess. It is essential to enjoy life and indulge in pleasures, but it is equally important to do so in moderation. Going to excess can lead to addiction, overspending, or overindulgence, which can be detrimental to our goals. With moderation restraint, we can maintain balance in our lives and avoid going overboard.

Limiting restraint involves the ability to set boundaries and limits for oneself. It is essential to know when to say no and avoid situations that may be harmful or detrimental to our goals. With limitation restraint, we can set boundaries for ourselves and avoid situations that may lead to negative consequences. Restraint is an essential component of Discipline, and unemotional, moderation, and limitation are three key elements of restraint that can help us maintain Discipline success. By practicing these skills, we can learn to control our emotions, avoid excess, and set boundaries for ourselves, which are all crucial for achieving our goals. With Discipline and restraint, we can overcome any obstacles that come our way and achieve the success we desire.

HOW HAVE I USED RESTRAINT AS RELATED TO DISCIPLINE IN MY LIFE:

The poignant narrative of my "Rose" experience embodies the essence of restraint as it intertwines with the concept of discipline. This life-altering journey, marked by profound loss and unexpected challenges, highlights the critical role of restraint in navigating emotionally charged situations with grace and strength. Restraint, in this context, was not just a passive withholding of reaction, but an active, disciplined choice to focus on what truly mattered: honoring Rose's memory and legacy.

This journey began with the devastating news of Rose's tragic passing, a moment that tested the limits of emotional endurance. The discipline to maintain composure and provide support to my grieving mother in that dire moment was a poignant demonstration of restraint. The treacherous drive to her location and the subsequent conversation where I had to deliver the heartbreaking news were acts that required a disciplined control over my emotions.

Organizing the Rose Pannone Memorial event further illustrated this concept of restraint in discipline. Here, the challenge was not just emotional but also logistical and administrative. The disciplined effort to coordinate with various stakeholders, amidst personal grief, showcased a restraint in managing emotions to achieve a significant goal—securing the future of Rose's children.

Moreover, the handling of Rose's estate as the administrator, a task fraught with legal complexities and financial challenges, demanded a high degree of restraint and discipline. It involved meticulous planning, clear-headed decision-making, and a steadfast commitment to ensuring the best for Rose's children, despite the emotional and bureaucratic hurdles.

Finally, the transformative moment at Rose's funeral, where I chose not to react impulsively to a hurtful rumor, was perhaps the most striking instance of restraint. It was a conscious decision to rise above the negativity and focus on the bigger picture, a discipline that has since reshaped my perspective on life.

In essence, my experience with Rose's passing and its aftermath is a profound testament to how restraint, when coupled with discipline, can guide us through life's most challenging moments. It demonstrates how these qualities enable us to honor our commitments, uphold our values, and emerge stronger, more centered, and more focused on what truly matters.

ROSE

"Rose died; Rose died!" My father cried on the cell phone.

It was a cold and snowy night on January 27, 2004. I was at home with my family when my phone rang. I answered it and heard my father's voice, trembling with grief and broken by sobs. "Rose è morta," Italian for "she died."

"Rose died!" Dad exclaimed. I felt a shock of disbelief and grief, I tried to process what he had just conveyed. My sister Rose had been involved in a fatal car accident.

Rose, my sister, was younger than me by five years, yet we shared a close bond. Named after our paternal grandmother, she was a caring single mother, devoted to her two beautiful children aged five and seven. Her determination to provide for them and create a good life was unwavering.

I couldn't believe that she was gone. I knew I had to deliver this devastating news to my mother. My parents were divorced, and they lived in different places. That night, my mother was house-sitting for a friend that night, and I understood the importance of facing her in person.

Driving through the treacherous, snow-covered roads, I focused solely on reaching her as swiftly as possible. Upon arriving at the house, she was watching, I knocked on the door, my urgency evident. Reluctance to open was understandable, given her solitude in an unfamiliar space. However, I persisted, shouting her name until she finally emerged.

"What's the matter?" she asked.

She could tell from my expression that something was wrong. Very wrong.

In the living room, I guided her to the couch, bracing myself for the most agonizing words I've ever spoken: "Rose died in a car accident, Mom." The silence hung heavy as the enormity of the tragedy settled in. Her anguished cry tore through the air, searing into my heart.

"Let's pray, Mom.", I said as I hugged her tightly.

With my arms around her, I offered solace through prayer. My mother's devout Christian faith and compassionate nature shone through as we sought strength for Rose's soul, her children, ourselves, and all who cherished her. That night, I insisted she stay with me; she wasn't alone in her grief.

Upon returning to my house, my young daughters awoke to our presence. The oldest, just four years old, inquired about Aunt Rose. "Daddy, what happened to Aunt Rose?"

"She is no longer with us," I said gently. "She passed away in an auto accident." My daughter looked confused and sad, but she didn't ask any more questions.

We all went to bed, but no-one slept well that night or many nights after. Rose's absence remained a poignant ache that reverberated through the nights. Her memory and the love we held for her endured, a testament to her enduring impact on her lives.

ROSE PANNONE MEMORIAL

Rose held a significance in my life that transcended the boundaries of sisterhood. Her bravery, compassion, and kindness served as a wellspring of inspiration. Through her infectious smile, unwavering happiness, and insightful wisdom, she left an indelible mark on the lives she touched. Following her passing, a profound emptiness took root within me. To honor her memory and provide support for her children, who had lost their mother, I initiated an event that aimed to celebrate her life and secure their educational and future needs.

I assembled a dedicated team of Rose's friends, family, and colleagues. We channeled our love for her and our shared determination into making the event successful. Leveraging the novel World Wide Web, we fashioned a website that paid homage to Rose while also promoting the event. Through letters and phone calls, we reached out to a multitude of individuals and organizations, requesting contributions and backing for our cause.

In an era before widespread email usage, we resorted to mailing hundreds of letters to various athletes, professional sports teams, celebrities, musicians, corporations, and any potential donors for our silent auction. The response was overwhelming, yielding a myriad of donations such as signed NFL helmets, photographs autographed by movie stars and athletes, CDs from renowned musicians, and posters from various sports leagues.

Our astonishment at the outpouring of support was palpable. The event, held on a sunny day in June at Rose's cherished park, drew over 200 attendees, comprising friends and family who gathered to commemorate her legacy. The occasion was adorned with food, music, games, entertainment, and heartfelt speeches from Rose's loved ones. The tangible success of the event translated into substantial funds raised for Rose's children's trust fund, an embodiment of the joy and love that Rose embodied.

The subsequent year's event encountered a less favorable outcome, marked by low attendance and negative profit. However, this setback failed to dishearten us. We recognized that our 2004 endeavor had achieved something extraordinary for Rose and her children. The inaugural event stands as an indelible memory for those who participated or bore witness, a testament to Rose's enduring spirit and legacy, eternally enshrined within our hearts.

The video of the event can be viewed at www.joeypinz.com

Reflecting on this journey, it's apparent that discipline and restraint were at play. The disciplined effort of assembling a team, reaching out for support, and organizing the event exemplified our commitment. Furthermore, the restraint to not be discouraged by the following year's challenge, but instead continue to honor Rose's legacy, underscores the enduring power of these qualities in the face of adversity.

ESTATE ADMINISTRATOR

Rose was my only sibling, employed by a prominent shipping company. As a single mother, she shouldered the responsibility of two children who relied on her entirely. Juggling the demands of providing for her children, Rose found herself with limited savings and no formal will in place.

Her untimely demise in a car accident struck me with an overwhelming sense of devastation, akin to losing a part of myself. Compounded by this loss was the burden of responsibility, I felt toward the children, now left without anyone to care for them. Eager to ensure her affairs were resolved and her children's future secured, I stepped forward as the administrator of her estate.

I soon realized that it was a challenging task. Navigating the judicial system became a necessity, compounded by the financial obligations that Rose had amassed over the years. Debts spanned from credit card dues to medical bills, utilities, and beyond. Her estate stood insolvent, unable to fulfill the obligations to her creditor due to insufficient funds.

I had to present an inventory of Rose's assets and liabilities. This experience was marked by a somber tone and a sense of humiliation. Adding to the distress, representatives from the state government claimed that Rose also owed back taxes. The ensuing mix of anger and helplessness surged within me. How could they demand money from someone who had nothing?

I was afraid that the proceeds from the fundraising event we had organized for Rose's children would have to be used to pay off her debt. The intention behind the event was to pay homage to Rose's life and empower her children, rather than catering to the desires of creditors. Thankfully, my lawyer told me that the event money was safe from any claims by debtors. He explained that since the event money was generated after Rose's death, it belonged solely to her children's trust fund, and no one else could touch it. This fact was a relief and a joy to me.

We had done something right for Rose and her children despite our challenges. We had raised enough money to ensure their education and well-being for years. We also beautifully honored Rose's memory. The fundraising event was one of the best things I ever did.

FUNERAL — A DRAMATIC SHIFT

Rose's funeral marked a profound turning point in my life, a moment that will always be etched in my memory. As I stood there with my notes in hand, ready to deliver a eulogy that would inspire people to do more, the enormity of the crowd struck me. The multitude present was a testament to the far-reaching impact Rose had on the world, and it was clear that her presence would be missed by many.

But amidst all the sorrow and grief, something shook me, a jarring encounter disrupted my thoughts. Someone approached me and shared a rumor about Rose's car accident, insinuating that her ex-boyfriend may have been involved. At that moment, I was filled with rage and incredulity. The insensitivity of bringing up a painful speculation at this moment was overwhelming. How could someone be so callous as to bring up such a hurtful rumor at a time like this?

But it was at that moment that I realized something truly powerful. I recognized the power of accepting that I couldn't control what people thought about me or the situations around me. And more importantly, it wasn't my responsibility to attempt such control. This epiphany marked the genesis of a significant shift in my mindset -from that day forward, I consciously stopped caring so much other people's thoughts. I focused on the handful of people whose opinions mattered to me and let go of the rest.

This attitude shift was genuinely liberating. It allowed me to let go of the need to judge others or worry about being judged myself. I felt free to be myself and to act in a way that was authentic to me rather than trying to fit into someone else's idea of who I should be.

I still carry this attitude with me to this day, and it's been one of the greatest gifts I've ever received. It's a reminder that life is too short to worry about what other people think. We should focus on the people we love, the things that matter to us, and living life to the fullest.

Rose may be gone, but her impact on my life will never be forgotten. She gave me the gift of liberation and the courage to be true to myself. For that, I will always be grateful. Thank you, Rose. I love and miss you. Your memory lives on in the lessons you've left behind.

This transformative experience underscores the significance of discipline and restraint. In the face of an unsettling moment during her funeral, I exercised restraint by not reacting impulsively to the hurtful rumor. I maintained discipline by staying true to the purpose of the eulogy and focusing on honoring Rose's memory. This example illustrates how these qualities can empower us to navigate challenges, center ourselves, and grow through adversity.

> *"Discipline and restraint are the foundation of a virtuous life. Discipline is the bridge that connects our goals to our achievements, while restraint is the key that unlocks the power of Discipline."*
> —Robin S. Sharm

DISCIPLINE ELEMENT LESSON LEARNED: RESTRAINT

There are many examples of Discipline in the passing of my sister. I showed great *restraint* when the person approached me with rumors before delivering the eulogy.

The powerful stories shared by my past podcast guests beautifully illustrate the role of restraint as an integral aspect of their disciplined lives. Just as my experience with Rose taught me the value of measured responses and focused intentions, these guests have also demonstrated how the practice of restraint can be a transformative tool in achieving personal and professional goals. Each guest, whether an artist managing creative impulses, a business leader making strategic decisions, or a social activist navigating complex social dynamics, has shown that restraint is often the silent yet potent force behind their successes. Their narratives reveal how disciplined restraint isn't about limiting oneself, but rather about channeling energy and emotions in a way that aligns with one's deeper values and objectives. Through their stories, we see the multifaceted role of restraint in discipline: as a means to maintain focus, to make thoughtful decisions, and to preserve integrity in the face of challenges.

JPDC GUEST: HUNTER

Hunter views restraint as something that he is capable of achieving due to his A-type personality, but he admits that he has suffered from attention deficit in the past. He credits yoga with helping him to develop Discipline and restrain his mind on what he wants to achieve. He believes consistent practice is essential for achieving results and that just doing it once is not enough. He also notes that some people come to yoga to learn how to bliss out and get out of their heads, but that yoga actually asks us to do the opposite—to come inward and concentrate our minds. Hunter considers concentration to be the greatest lesson that yoga teaches us.

JPDC GUEST: ODIN

Odin perceives restraint as an important element of success. He advocates getting out of one's comfort zone, being more fearless, and maintaining a strong sense of focus. This mindset guided him in crafting his book, which he then shared with a sizable audience of 500 attorneys during a conference. He also talks about the importance of restraint in his personal and professional life. Odin highlights the transformative impact of his involvement in the entrepreneur's organization, detailing how it facilitated significant outcomes such as securing a mortgage through an EO member, enlisting the guidance of a scaling up coach, and collaborating with an executive coach.

For Odin, the crux lies in the notion that what receives our attention tends to flourish. He underscores the value of concentrating on the underlying thought processes that drive outcomes, rather than solely fixating on end results. He emphasizes the need to be an active participant to get the most out of an organization.

JPDC GUEST: CLAIR

Clair delves into the concept of restraint across various aspects of her life. In terms of her career aspirations, she mentions her intense involvement in marketing, with a primary emphasis on aiding sports teams. However, she also admits to having moments where she questions what she's doing and whether it will work, but she tries to stay calm and push through.

In terms of her current involvement with a soccer team, Clair's primary objective is to assist them in maintaining their position in the league. She underscores the importance of Discipline and the ability to effectively separate her focus between her company and her football training.

Overall, it seems that Clair values restraint as an important tool for achieving her goals and staying on track.

JPDC GUEST: ANTHONY

Anthony holds restraint as an essential factor in achieving goals and Attaining accomplishments. His perspective on life is all encompassing, underlined by his affiliation with the Muslim faith, which places great importance on Discipline and adhering to principles. He shares how the power of Discipline played a pivotal role in his personal growth.

Additionally, Anthony highlights that focus and Discipline need to be aligned with a clear moral vision to be effective. He also talks about the Prophet Muhammad, who he considers the most influential person in history. Anthony emphasizes that the Prophet's personality was genuine and true to his beliefs without any dichotomy between church and state.

3-OBEDIENCE

> *"Discipline and obedience are the twin pillars of success. Without discipline there would be no obedience, and without obedience, there can be no Discipline."*
> —Stephen Covey

We view Obedience as acting on the orders of an authority figure, a form of social influence that differs from compliance and conformity, and as controlled behavior, self-control. Some synonyms for obedience are:

- Compliance
- Dutifulness
- Submissiveness
- Acquiescence
- Tractability

Obedience is a noun that means "the act of obeying; dutiful or submissive behavior with respect to another person" or "the trait of being willing to obey. "Some examples of Obedience are:

- Being Obedient to the family head: In a family, the junior members should obey the senior ones. It is the duty of every child to obey his parents.
- Being obedient to the government laws: The government enjoins some laws and rules for the maintenance of peace and security of the state. The citizens should obey these laws for their welfare.
- Being obedient to God: For Christians, obedience to God is an act of worship and a way of following Jesus' example and commands. They believe that God's will is good and perfect for them.

Obedience stands as a vital facet of Discipline, encompassing the adherence to regulations and the recognition of authority. This skill is instrumental in achieving success across a spectrum of life domains, spanning personal relationships to professional careers. The concept of Obedience can be broken down into three fundamental aspects: compliance, dutifulness, and submissiveness.

Compliance is the ability to adhere to established rules and regulations. It plays a pivotal role within the realm of Discipline by facilitating the navigation of social dynamics and averting conflicts. With compliance, we can adhere to laws and regulations, follow ethical norms, execute instructions and demonstrate respect for the rights of others.

Dutifulness encapsulates the aptitude to fulfill obligations and responsibilities. Fueled by a sense of duty, this trait propels us to meet our expectations and responsibilities. Through dutifulness, we effectively engage in our roles as citizens, employees, and family members, contributing positively to the community.

Submissiveness revolves around the willingness to yield to authoritative figures. It involves embracing decisions made by individuals in positions of power, such as supervisors, educators, or government representatives. By practicing submissiveness, we open ourselves to learning from those with greater experience, thereby benefiting from their insights and guidance.

In the grand tapestry of Discipline, obedience constitutes an indispensable thread.

Compliance, dutifulness, and submissiveness form the triad of obedience, guiding us in navigating social dynamics, fulfilling responsibilities, and tapping into the wisdom of authority figures. Through cultivating obedience, we develop the capacity to uphold regulations, meet obligations, and uphold the rights of others. This, in turn, enables us to attain success across various facets of life while making positive contributions to society.

HOW HAVE I USED OBEDIENCE AS RELATED TO DISCIPLINE IN MY LIFE:

The experience of my parents' divorce and its aftermath serves as a poignant example of how obedience, interwoven with discipline, played a crucial role in navigating through a significant life transition. The decision to live primarily with my mother and sister was not just a choice of residence, but a step into a realm of increased responsibility and an implicit obedience to the needs of my family unit. This act of obedience was guided by a disciplined understanding of the situation's demands and the roles I needed to play.

In taking on a leadership role within the family, I was adhering to an unspoken obligation to support and guide my younger sister and to assist my mother. This obedience was not passive submission but a conscious, disciplined choice to prioritize the well-being of my family over personal comfort or freedom. This period of my life taught me the delicate balance between leveraging personal freedoms and privileges for my benefit while maintaining a disciplined approach to family responsibilities.

This experience parallels the stories shared by my podcast guests, where obedience, coupled with discipline, has been a key factor in their personal and professional development. Like my own experience, their journeys often involved making tough choices that required adherence to certain principles or responsibilities, whether in their careers, personal lives, or creative endeavors. Obedience, in this sense, is a disciplined commitment to a cause, a role, or a set of values, driving them to overcome obstacles and achieve their goals.

DIVORCE

When I turned twelve, my parents made the difficult decision to get divorced. This had a profound impact on my seven-year-old sister, who struggled to cope with the changes. As the older sibling, I was faced with a pivotal choice when my mother asked me who I wanted to live with primarily. I opted to stay with her and my sister, and we settled into a cozy apartment within a house that housed friendly individuals from my mother's church community.

During this period, I began to realize the distinct role I played as the only male in the household. Our living arrangements were tight, with my mother and sister sharing bunk beds in a single bedroom, while I slept on a fold-out couch in the living room. This unique situation naturally led me to take on a leadership role within the family.

My parents granted me certain privileges due to my status as the oldest child, and I learned to leverage them effectively. This skillful manipulation of my circumstances allowed me to navigate challenges and yield positive results. I grasped the importance of adaptability and flexibility to steer situations towards favorable outcomes.

One significant aspect of this period was how I harnessed my parents' divorce as an opportunity for my benefit. Whenever I encountered trouble with one parent, I would seek refuge at the other's home, cleverly navigating the situation to my advantage. This experience instilled a robust work ethic in me, as I recognized the need for finances to pursue my desires. This early encounter with discipline and responsibility ignited my resourcefulness and turned my freedom into a tool for creating opportunities.

Amidst these personal dynamics, my passion for both sports and music deepened. Engaging in soccer at various levels, from local teams to travel and club squads, occupied much of my time. Simultaneously, music played a significant role in my life. My mother's collection boasted timeless artists like the Beatles, Chuck Berry, Beach Boys, Ray Charles, Simon and Garfunkel, and Little Richard. However, I also embraced my generation's music, reveling in the sounds of Duran Duran, Prince, Met at Work, Styx, Kool and the Gang, Hall & Oates, Michael Jackson, Madonna, and U2.

This phase of my life, defined by my parents' divorce, became an invaluable lesson in capitalizing on prevailing circumstances and transforming them into opportunities. It marked the outset of my journey into leadership, where I embraced responsibility within my household. Looking back, I recognize the growth and resilience that emerged from this challenging time, teaching me to stand on my own feet, work diligently, and approach life with a disciplined mindset.

> *"Discipline is the foundation upon which all success is built. Obedience is the cornerstone of Discipline"*
> —J. Krishnamurti

DISCIPLINE ELEMENT LESSON LEARNED: OBEDIENCE

While capitalizing on the family issues, I arranged and compiled new rules and remained *obedient*.

The compelling stories of obedience intertwined with discipline, shared by my podcast guests, mirror the complexities and growth I experienced during my parents' divorce. Just as I navigated the intricacies of family dynamics with a disciplined approach to obedience, these guests have shown how this quality can be a potent force in their journeys. Each guest, in their respective fields, has demonstrated the importance of adhering to certain principles, guidelines, or external expectations, not as a surrender of autonomy, but as a strategic and disciplined choice to advance their goals. Whether it was an artist complying with the rigorous demands of their craft, a business leader following ethical standards in decision-making, or an athlete adhering to strict training regimens, their stories highlight obedience as a form of disciplined commitment. This disciplined obedience, far from being a mere submission, is a conscious decision to align one's actions with larger objectives, showcasing how it can be a powerful tool in achieving success and personal growth.

JPDC GUEST: JOSEPHINE

Josephine views obedience as essential for keeping the business going, especially during stress or challenges. She believes that it's crucial to focus and exercise restraint on the core strengths and gifts you bring to the company. Simultaneously, it's essential to delegate other tasks to the team. By doing this, you can grow the company and identify new opportunities that you might have missed if you were too obedient to the minutiae of day-to-day tasks.

JPDC GUEST: GABRIEL

According to Gabriel's viewpoint, obedience plays a pivotal role in effectively managing a thriving business. He believes that artists who focus only on their art and neglect the business side often struggle financially. Gabriel introduces the 80/20 rule, which suggests that 80 percent of your results come from 20 percent of your efforts. This underscores the significance of prioritizing critical tasks. Additionally, Gabriel acknowledges that it can be challenging to break the habit of trying to do too many things simultaneously. He observes that individuals often fall into the trap of feeling like they're not working hard enough if they only focus on a few tasks.

JPDC Guest: Autumn

Autumn views focus as a form of obedience that leads to success in her business. She has learned how to systemize her workflow and delegate tasks. This approach enables her to concentrate predominantly on the artistic realm of floral design in her business. By automating the booking process for most clients, she can easily delegate tasks to others. This strategy permits her to limit the number of one-on-one clients she works with to twelve per year. This intentional restraint ensures that Autumn remains artistically fulfilled while dedicating her time to crafting significant and extraordinary floral arrangements.

She uses the obedience of enlisting a bookkeeper and accountant to oversee other aspects of her business. This deliberate choice liberates her to focus on her core expertise. In essence, Autumn's approach underscores the value of harnessing her strengths and entrusting certain tasks to others, ultimately cultivating a conducive environment for her creative endeavors.

JPDC GUEST: SOPHIE

Sophie discusses her commitment to practicing embodiment and how it influenced her decision to relocate to Australia to establish a fresh way of living. She reflects on the early lesson she learned about suppressing her authentic self, leading her to develop disordered eating habits. Eventually, she identified this behavior as a manifestation of a victim mentality.

4-MASTERY

> "Discipline is the path to mastery; the more we Discipline ourselves to do what is right and necessary, the closer we come to mastering our craft."
> —Robert Greene

We view mastery as comprehensive knowledge or skill in a subject or accomplishment. Also, control or superiority over someone or something.

Examples of Mastery are:

- Time management, focus, interaction, and a positive attitude
- Doing the right things and avoiding the nonpositive
- Recognizing our prejudices
- Controlling what you think and what you do
- Being patient and persistent

Mastery is a critical aspect of Discipline that involves the ability to become proficient in a particular skill or field. It is a crucial skill that can help us succeed in our personal and professional lives. Mastery can be broken down into three key elements: proficiency, skill, and expertise. Proficiency involves the ability to perform a particular task with ease and accuracy. It is the foundation of mastery, achieved through practice and repetition. With proficiency, we can improve our work, complete tasks more quickly, and produce higher-quality results.

Some synonyms to Mastery in pertaining to Discipline are:
- Skill
- Expertise
- Proficiency
- Command
- Prowess

Skill involves the ability to apply knowledge and proficiency to real-world situations. It is the ability to adapt to new challenges and solve problems creatively. With skill, we can handle complex tasks, make informed decisions, and navigate difficult situations with ease.

Expertise involves the ability to become a recognized authority in a particular field or industry. It is achieved through years of experience and continuous learning. With expertise, we can provide valuable insights and guidance to others, contribute to our field in meaningful ways, and achieve success at the highest levels.

Mastery is an essential component of the Discipline. Proficiency, skill, and expertise are three key elements of mastery that can help succeed in our personal and professional lives. By practicing and refining our skills, we can become more proficient in our work, apply our knowledge to real-world situations, and become recognized authorities in our fields. With mastery, we can achieve our goals, contribute to society in meaningful ways, and lead fulfilling lives.

HOW HAVE I USED MASTERY AS RELATED TO DISCIPLINE IN MY LIFE:

The rich tapestry of my "New York City Origins" and the diverse backgrounds of my parents encapsulate the essence of mastery as it relates to discipline. Just as my father and mother harnessed their respective hardships and cultural influences to build a life in a new land, mastery in the context of discipline often involves the skilled navigation of life's complexities and the ability to adapt and thrive in varied circumstances. My parents' journey, marked by resilience and a strong work ethic, exemplifies a mastery of life's challenges, achieved through disciplined perseverance and adaptability.

In the same vein, my podcast guests have shared stories where mastery, intertwined with discipline, played a pivotal role in their successes. These individuals, from vastly different backgrounds and professions, have each honed their skills and knowledge through a disciplined approach to their crafts. Whether it was an artist mastering intricate techniques, a scientist persistently pursuing groundbreaking research, or an entrepreneur navigating the complexities of the business world, their stories underscore how mastery is not just about innate talent but also the disciplined application and refinement of skills over time. These narratives illustrate that mastery, much like the story of my family, is achieved through a combination of disciplined effort, continuous learning, and the resilience to overcome obstacles.

NEW YORK CITY ORIGINS

How My Parents' Backgrounds Influenced My Life

My parents have very different backgrounds that shaped their lives and personalities. They met in Queens, New York City, in 1966, but they came from very different places and cultures.

My father was born in southern Italy, where his family eked out a living as garbanzo bean farmers. His poor upbringing was marked by scarcity, and he didn't own a pair of shoes until the age of twelve, reserving them solely for church visits. His mother's apprehensions about potential drafts led them to Switzerland post-World War II. His father's unfulfilled promises of support following a government lottery victory for farming land in Argentina resulted in abandonment. Consequently, my father faced numerous hardships and grew up without a paternal figure. His persistence propelled him through welding school in Switzerland, where he encountered both discrimination and harsh winters. The generosity of the nuns who offered him a coat provided a glimmer of solace. At eighteen, he managed to migrate to New York City, seizing opportunities as a welder and eventually becoming a U.S. Citizen.

On the other hand, my mother's origins can be traced to Nova Scotia, Canada. Her family also engaged in farming and possessed a strong work ethic and devout Catholic beliefs, they were French-speaking and had many children. My grandfather, an adept carpenter, imparted invaluable skills to me. Economic constraints prompted their relocation to New York City, following in the footsteps of relatives who had already settled there.

In the heart of Flushing, Queens, my parents found love and married. My birthplace was New Haven, Connecticut, a reflection of my father's uncle's migration. While Connecticut became my primary residence, frequent visits to New York City allowed me to connect with relatives and explore the city's diverse offerings.

My upbringing was profoundly influenced by my parents' multifaceted backgrounds. Their teachings instilled in me resilience, a strong work ethic, and adaptability. Exposure to diverse cultures, languages, and traditions broadened my horizons, cultivating a rich sense of history, family, and identity. These influences have collectively contributed to shaping my present self.

Our family's narrative is a living testament to the embodiment of the American dream. The story underscores the potential of hard work, unwavering perseverance, and resolute determination to surmount formidable challenges. It serves as a poignant reminder that our heritage and lineage can serve as foundational guides, but ultimately, it's our choices and actions that steer the course of our lives.

My family's story is a testament to the American dream, where hard work, perseverance, and determination can overcome even the greatest obstacles. It is a reminder that our roots and heritage can shape our lives, but ultimately, it is our choices and actions that determine our destiny.

> *"Discipline is the bridge between goals and accomplishment, and mastery is the destination at the end of the bridge."*
> —John C. Maxwell

DISCIPLINE ELEMENT LESSON LEARNED: MASTERY

My parents instilled in me the value of hard work to achieve my goals. While I might not possess the same level of natural intelligence as some, I believe that dedicating myself to diligent effort and developing expertise in a particular field will lead me to success.

The fascinating journeys of mastery intertwined with discipline, as shared by my past podcast guests, echo the intricate blend of cultural richness and resilience found in my "New York City Origins." Each guest, in mastering their respective fields, has demonstrated how disciplined dedication to their craft is essential in achieving excellence. Whether it was a musician perfecting their art through countless hours of practice, a business leader continually refining their strategies in the dynamic world of commerce, or an athlete rigorously training to reach peak performance, the theme of mastery through discipline is a common thread in their stories. These individuals have shown that mastery is not a destination, but a continuous journey marked by disciplined effort, persistent learning, and an unwavering commitment to excel in their chosen paths.

Their experiences offer a vivid illustration of how mastery, achieved through disciplined practice and perseverance, can lead to remarkable achievements and personal fulfillment.

JPDC GUEST: BATHSHEBA

Bathsheba views mastery as a crucial aspect of being an entrepreneur or coach. She distinguishes between knowing how to *do* something and knowing how to *be* something, suggesting that true mastery requires not just technical knowledge but also a deeper understanding of oneself and one's energy. Bathsheba believes that the path to mastery is not always straightforward and that many struggle with trying multiple modalities without success. However, she also suggests that mastery can be achieved through simplicity and understanding the underlying principles that govern our lives. Bathsheba mentions introducing "woo-woo" (presumably referring to spiritual or metaphysical practices) into her work, indicating that she sees value in exploring non-traditional methods to help her clients achieve mastery. Overall, Bathsheba seems to view mastery as an ongoing journey that requires a combination of technical skill, self-awareness, and an openness to new approaches.

JPDC GUEST: AUBREY

Aubrey sees self-mastery as a foundational element, considering it crucial to comprehend oneself comprehensively, including biologically and neurologically. She asserts that grasping what causes unhappiness, how one reacts, and recognizing fears and weaknesses is essential. In her view, the modern world lacks the daily challenges our ancestors encountered, leading to an inflated sense of competence and a lack of meaningful challenges.

JPDC GUEST: ANDRES

Andres views mastery as a key to becoming very efficient at a specific skill. He emphasizes that focusing on one thing and becoming very good at it, one can become more efficient and productive, which allows them to deliver more output in the same amount of time. According to Andres, by practicing the same skill repeatedly, one can achieve a level of mastery that makes them more effective and efficient at their work.

JPDC GUEST: MICAH

Micah considers mastery an essential aspect of their work in digital marketing. They focus on data-driven strategies, analyzing conversion rates, media buying costs, and click-through rates to identify what works and doesn't. They also emphasize the importance of testing and experimentation to find new ways to scale and drive growth. Micah believes that having a clear understanding of the KPIs and goals of a campaign is crucial to maintaining focus and achieving success. He also notes that different roles within marketing require different skill sets, so there may be separate individuals responsible for generating leads and closing sales.

5-CONTROL

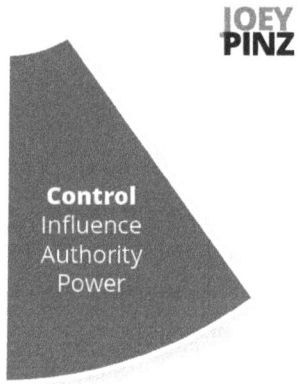

> *By constant self-Discipline and self-control, you can develop greatness of character.*
> *—Grenville Kleiser*

We see 'control' as governing the situation. It signifies being the decision-maker or having the ability to regulate the essential elements. For instance:

- The driver of the car exhibited full control of the vehicle.
- He lost control of his car and crashed into a tree.
- She was appointed to control the company's marketing strategy.
- The city wanted local control of education.
- Keeping dogs demands the capability to control their behavior.

Focus on what you can control, not on what you can't control. Some synonyms of "control" are:

- Influence
- Authority

- Power
- Manage
- Limit

The concept of control is an integral part of discipline. Control can be understood as the ability to manage your actions, thoughts, and emotions to achieve a desired outcome. It is a skill that enables us to focus our energies in the right direction and thereby be disciplined in our approach to life. Discipline, at its core, is the practice of making choices that are aligned with your goals and values, and control is a vital component of this practice.

Control can manifest in various forms and aspects of life—self-control, emotional control, control over your time, and even control over your environment. When it comes to discipline, self-control is perhaps the most immediate form that comes to mind. It involves the ability to resist immediate gratification in favor of long-term gains. Whether choosing to exercise rather than Instagram or opting for a nutritious meal over fast food, self-control forms the backbone of a disciplined lifestyle.

Control over one's time is another dimension of discipline. Time management is not merely about allocating specific blocks of time to tasks but involves the control to adhere to those time blocks rigorously. The ability to control distractions and focus on the task is an essential element of time-related discipline. Without control, even the best-laid plans will fall apart, rendering your disciplined approach ineffective.

Control also involves managing your environment to foster discipline. This means creating spaces that are conducive to focus and concentration, thereby facilitating a disciplined routine. Whether it's your workspace, home, or even the company you keep, having control over these environments can substantially impact your level of discipline.

The element of control is not just a one-dimensional concept but a multi-faceted skill that affects various aspects of discipline.

It forms the structural framework upon which discipline is built. Whether it's controlling your immediate desires, managing your emotional responses, adhering to a structured timetable, or shaping your environment, control is the underlying force that enables us to lead a disciplined life. It allows us to channel our efforts effectively toward achieving our goals, thereby fulfilling the broader vision of personal and societal betterment through discipline.

HOW HAVE I USED CONTROL AS RELATED TO DISCIPLINE IN MY LIFE:

The narrative of my "I'm Fat! And Going to Die!" experience poignantly illustrates the concept of control as it intersects with discipline. This personal journey, marked by a confronting realization of my health and well-being, mirrors the essential discipline of exerting control over one's life choices and actions. Much like the focused effort required to address my health concerns, control in the realm of discipline involves the conscious regulation of behavior, decisions, and habits to align with desired outcomes. It's about taking charge of one's path, making deliberate choices, and consistently applying the self-discipline needed to follow through with those decisions. This story is a testament to the fact that while we cannot control every aspect of our lives, the disciplined control we do have can be a powerful tool in transforming our health, mindset, and ultimately, our lives.

I'M FAT! AND GOING TO DIE!

What have I done to myself?

I saw pictures of myself at 340 pounds, a weight categorized as 'obese' according to the body mass index (BMI) calculator. Nonetheless, I disagree with using BMI as the sole indicator of obesity, especially for athletes with substantial muscle mass. This measurement can misrepresent health, as many athletes with low body fat might be inaccurately classified as obese due to their height-based calculations. For example, many athletes with <10 percent body fat would be considered obese.

Obesity is a serious health condition that can increase the risk of developing various diseases and complications, such as:

- Heart disease and strokes: Obesity can raise my blood pressure and cholesterol levels, risk factors for heart disease and strokes.
- Type 2 diabetes: Obesity can make my body resistant to insulin, a hormone that regulates blood sugar levels. This can lead to type 2 diabetes, which can damage my organs and nerves.
- Sleep apnea: Obesity can cause excess fat around my neck, which can block my airway during sleep. This can lead to sleep apnea, a disorder that causes me to stop repeatedly breathing during sleep. This can affect my quality of sleep and increase my risk of heart problems.
- Certain cancers: Obesity can cause hormonal changes and inflammation in my body, which can promote the growth of abnormal cells. This can increase my risk of certain cancers, such as breast, colon, gallbladder, pancreatic, kidney, and prostate cancer.

Making a significant change in one's life can be a daunting task, especially when it involves health and wellness. My personal journey of shedding weight and embracing a healthier lifestyle serves as inspiration to many. Seeing my 340-pound images triggered a realization: it was time to regain control of my life.

What stands out from my journey is that I was not looking for a temporary fix; I wanted a full lifestyle change. It is easy to fall into the trap of fad diets that promise quick results, but I recognized that it takes a holistic approach to achieve lasting changes in one's health and well-being. My determination to keep my plans private—I did not seek validation or support from anyone else, and I had a great fear of failure—underscores my individual determination and resilience in pursuing this change.

Daily workouts at a local gym became a cornerstone. I joined a local gym and worked out every day without fail for eight months, doing cardio and weights. Waking up at 5 am to work out every day for eight months takes Discipline and a strong will. This routine laid the groundwork for my day and cultivated my focus, dedication, and commitment. I explored different workout options, such as cycling and spin classes, and watched TV shows and movies while on the elliptical machine and found creative ways to stay engaged. I was not going to let anything stand in my way of achieving your goals.

My story can be a testament to the power of commitment and perseverance. I took ownership of my health and wellness and made a conscious decision to change my lifestyle. I understood it was a long-term journey, and I was prepared to put in the effort and dedication required to achieve my goals. My journey can be an inspiration to many who are struggling with their health and well-being, and it shows that with Discipline, commitment, and hard work, anything is possible.

HOW I CHANGED MY LIFE BY LOSING WEIGHT

Many people struggle with their weight and health issues. I was one of them. I used to carry a weight of 340 pounds, a burden that left me feeling unhappy, unhealthy, and unattractive. I knew I had to make a change for myself and my daughter, so I embarked on a journey to share how I changed my life by shedding weight. The first step I took was to decide to change my lifestyle. I did not want to go on some temporary diet that would only make me gain back weight later. I wanted to adopt new habits that would last for a lifetime. I wanted to eat better, exercise more, and care for myself.

The second step I took was to join a local gym and work out every day without fail for eight months. I did cardio and weights, tailored to my mood and energy level. The early morning, around 5 am, proved ideal, ensuring accomplishments, and setting a positive tone for the day.

The third step I took was to *enjoy* the process and the results. Working out became fun for me, as I watched many great series and movies on the DVD players on the elliptical machines. Engaging in cycling and spin classes added challenge and sweat, contributing to a visibly stronger, leaner, and healthier body. The fourth step I took was to keep my goal a secret, sharing it only with my daughter. Perhaps I did not want them to know in case I failed, or perhaps, I wanted them to be surprised by my transformation. Either way, I felt that this was something I had to do for myself, not for anyone else. I got myself into this mess, and darn it, I would get myself out of it!

Through this journey, I learned many valuable lessons. I learned how to be dedicated, committed, and Disciplined. I learned how to love myself, respect myself, and appreciate myself. I learned how to be happy, healthy, and confident.

Losing weight changed my life in many ways. It improved my physical health, my mental health, and my self-esteem. It made me proud of myself and inspired others around me. It made me a better person and a better father.

Losing weight was not easy, but it was worth it. It was the best decision I ever made in my life.

HOW I LOST WEIGHT BY CHANGING THE FOOD & BEVERAGES I CONSUMED.

BEVERAGES

Once, I used to indulge in the habit of consuming heavy-caloric beverages, particularly numerous cans of soda each day. Realizing the unhealthiness of this practice, I acknowledged the negative impact of sugar-based calories on both my well-being and calorie intake. My objective was clear: cut down on calories, with beverages being a significant contributor.

The realization that a single can of soda contains about 130 calories was a significant turning point for me. I knew I needed to find a healthier alternative that would still quench my thirst and provide me with the necessary fluids my body required. After much thought and research, I decided to make green tea my go-to beverage.

Green tea, recognized for its health benefits, including being a natural antioxidant and aiding in weight loss, stood out as an ideal replacement for soda. Its low-calorie count made it a perfect fit. I initiated with one daily cup of green tea, and gradually I increased the number of cups until I was drinking close to a gallon of green tea a day.

I found that green tea had a satisfying taste and provided me with the necessary hydration my body needed. I also realized that green tea gave me a boost of energy that lasted throughout the day. I began to feel healthier, and my body began to feel more energized as well.

Along with drinking green tea, I also incorporated water into my daily routine. I made sure to drink at least eight glasses of water per day, which not only kept me hydrated but also helped in flushing out toxins from my body.

An interesting fact is that I have never had a cup of coffee. I have always preferred tea over coffee, and my preference for green tea has further reinforced this. I am glad that I have found a healthier alternative to soda, and I plan to continue to drink green tea and water to maintain my healthy lifestyle.

FOOD

Losing weight is a difficult journey for many people, especially those who love to cook and eat, like me. As a lover of pizza, Italian cuisine, hamburgers, and all kinds of food, I found it challenging to change my eating habits. However, I knew I needed to change what I ate to lose weight and improve my health.

I started by acknowledging that I still needed these foods in my life, but in smaller portions. Instead of eating a whole pizza, I ate half, and instead of two cheeseburgers, I ate one. I realized that removing these foods from my life would only lead to me returning to them and gaining weight back. Therefore, I decided to make a complete life change, not a temporary one.

I understood that over 90 percent of people who lose dramatic weight gain it back within a year. I did not want to be part of this statistic as this would do untold damage to my body. My goal was to get off all the pills I had been prescribed due to my new obesity, and I knew that changing my eating habits was a crucial step toward achieving this goal.

I also incorporated healthier foods into my diet, such as lean proteins, whole grains, fruits, and vegetables. I learned how to cook healthy meals that were delicious and satisfying. I started to look at food as fuel for my body rather than just something to enjoy.

It was not easy to change my eating habits, but I knew it was necessary to achieve my goals. I also decided to stop relying on body mass index (BMI) to measure being overweight. As an athlete with big muscular soccer legs, my BMI did not accurately represent my body composition. Instead, I focused on how I felt and how my clothes fit.

Overall, changing what I ate was a significant factor in my weight loss journey. By cutting portions, incorporating healthier foods, and making a complete life change, I was able to achieve my goals and improve my health.

INTERMITTENT FASTING

I have been practicing intermittent fasting for a couple of years. On a typical day, I only eat two meals a day. My eating window typically starts around noon after not consuming calories for about 16 hours, including evening hours. As a non-coffee drinker, I've gone without calories for up to 48 hours (about 2 days). Contrary to how it may appear, this practice is not as difficult as it seems.

7 MONTHS

This photo captures all the clothes I had to give away after losing all the weight. I decided to part with my "fat" clothes, as I knew I would never need them again since I was committed to NEVER being that weight again! Losing weight can be a challenging journey for many people, and it certainly was for me.

Within seven months, I lost one hundred pounds, but it was a slow burn-off. I noticed that my clothes became loose on me and no longer fit. However, I still had more work to do. At 230 pounds, I knew that I still had more weight to lose.

I started to dive deeper into my eating habits and calorie intake. I was shocked to learn that a dry bagel was 330 calories! How many more calories was I consuming, unaware? I decided to keep my daily calorie intake under two thousand calories daily.

I also started to incorporate more protein into my diet and began consuming five meals throughout the day. My routine consisted of three small meals and two snacks throughout the day. I drank plenty of water and avoided eating anything past six or seven pm.

Losing weight was not easy, but I was determined to succeed. I found that having a support system was crucial, and I surrounded myself with people who encouraged and motivated me. I also found it helpful to track my progress and celebrate every small victory along the way.

Although those around me only slightly noticed my weight loss since they saw me often, my friends who hadn't seen me for months noticed and complimented me. Their recognition of my progress motivated me to continue on my weight loss journey.

Overall, losing weight was a challenging yet rewarding experience for me. By monitoring my calorie intake, incorporating more protein, and eating five times a day, I was able to lose weight and improve my health. It took hard work and dedication, but I am grateful for my progress and the healthier lifestyle I have adopted.

TRIATHLON

I was acquainted with triathlons through reading and decided to pursue them as a fitness challenge. Given my dislike for running, I opted against marathons and instead focused on swimming and cycling, both of which I enjoyed. The motivation behind engaging in triathlons was to shed weight, enhance fitness, and stimulate both physical and mental growth. Triathlons are multisport events that consist of swimming, cycling, and running in succession. They require endurance, strength, speed, agility, and coordination.

Some of the benefits of doing triathlons are:

- Comprehensive workout: Triathlons engage all the major muscle groups -swimming for upper body strength, cycling for lower body toning, and running for lean muscle development. They also improve cardiovascular health by increasing my heart rate and blood circulation.
- Weight Loss: Triathlons burn many calories because they involve three different activities that use different energy systems. They also boost metabolism and help build lean muscle mass, which burns more calories at rest.

- Cognitive health: Triathlons challenged my brain with various skills and strategies, as well as triggering the release of endorphins, which contribute to feelings of happiness and stress reduction.
- Bone health: The exertion of triathlons reinforced my bones, enhancing density and strength. The activities also enhanced balance and flexibility, reducing risks of fractures.

These benefits motivated me to pursue triathlons for weight loss and fitness. I initiated training for swimming, biking and running. I engaged a coach to improve my swimming technique, found access through a local master's program, and soon developed a genuine fondness for swimming. Cycling wasn't challenging but required financial investment for a decent road bike. The advantage of road biking lies in the even power of distribution between upstrokes and downstrokes due to clipped shoes. The time-consuming nature of road biking, though less physically demanding than swimming or running, posed a challenge.

As a soccer player, running held negative associations due to its punitive use by inferior coaches. Overcoming this, I paid attention to proper running form and hydration. With a weight of 230 pounds, the strain on my body was a concern. My first goal was to finish an Olympic triathlon, comprising a .9-mile swim, a 25-mile bike, and a 6.4-mile run. My goal was to finish. No particular time. Just finish.

My dedication led me to complete my first triathlon. Subsequently, I participated in more Olympic and sprint triathlons, halved versions of the Olympic distance. Eventually, I aimed to finish in under four hours and incorporated CrossFit into my routine. Convincing friends to join me, we ventured into triathlons together. When I reached the finish line, my official time was 3 hours 59 minutes. I beat my goal by seconds. The journey showcased my determination and the significant strides I had made.

> "Discipline is the key to control. When we
> Discipline ourselves to do what is necessary,
> we gain control over our lives."
> —Brian Tracy

DISCIPLINE ELEMENT LESSON LEARNED: CONTROL

Perhaps the most remarkable feat in my life is losing and keeping off all the weight I put on. I had to continue to take *control* of my health.

My weight loss journey has taught me invaluable lessons about Discipline and control. I've come to realize that quick fixes aren't sustainable; instead, embracing long-term lifestyle changes demands a strong sense of control. By managing my portion sizes, meticulously tracking my calorie intake, and sticking to a consistent meal schedule, I've seen firsthand how Discipline shapes my choices and habits.

Building a support system has shown me the power of seeking encouragement externally to strengthen my sense of control. Regularly assessing my progress and focusing on personal milestones underscore how Discipline fuels ongoing self-improvement. Incorporating physical activity into my routine and celebrating each achievement highlights the importance of consistent effort and positive reinforcement. My journey has illuminated that through control, guided by Discipline, I've been able to drive enduring, transformative changes that extend to my choices, daily routines, and overall mindset.

JPDC GUEST: BROOKLYN

Brooklyn views control as something that should not be oppressive and stifling. She argues that command and control leadership hamper creative innovation. Instead, she advocates for servant leadership, where leaders support and nurture their teams to contribute their best work. Brooklyn sees leadership as guiding teams toward a shared vision, ensuring their well-being and growth. Management, on the other hand, involves resource allocation and control. Brooklyn' stance underscores the idea that control should be used to support and empower others rather than exerting authority over them.

JPDC GUEST: BATHSHEBA

Bathsheba sees control as an aspect she refrains from labeling explicitly. Instead, she considers it the utilization of her mental faculties –mind, imagination, and intuition –to steer her decision-making. She underscores Discipline's role in evolving her approach by posing distinct questions than before. Rather than reacting impulsively, she responds by asking herself if she wants to be involved with a particular project or person and if it adds value to her or not. Bathsheba emphasizes the importance of being 100 percent present and giving her all in everything she does rather than just going through the motions.

JPDC GUEST: ANTHONY

According to Anthony, control holds a crucial place within the spiritual Discipline of Islam. He highlights that intentions drive actions, and God's rewards or penalties align with these deeds. Therefore, controlling one's inner desires and impulses is essential to avoid committing sins. Anthony also emphasizes Prophet Muhammad disciplined life in both personal and public spheres. He posits that discipline is key for self-control and asserts that Islam offers avenues for spiritual Discipline.

JPDC GUEST: ANDRES:

Andres stresses the significance of assuming responsibility and managing one's life while crafting a strategy to live congruently with one's purpose. He places importance on possessing a feeling of control, direction, and agency in one's life.

6-ROUTINE

> "Discipline is the foundation upon which all success is built. Routine is the vehicle that takes us there."
> —Jocko Willink

A 'routine' refers to a regular sequence of actions or behaviors that are performed consistently over time. Some examples of 'routine' are:

- Waking up at 5 AM every day and going for a morning run.
- Following a specific skincare regimen involving cleansing, toning, and moisturizing every night.
- Starting the workday with a review of emails and planning tasks for the day.
- Practicing a musical instrument for 30 minutes every evening.
- Have a set bedtime routine that includes reading for 20 minutes before turning off the lights.

Some synonyms of routine are:
- Procedure
- Practice
- Pattern
- Drill
- Regime

Some points of routine:

Routine, as it pertains to Discipline, is a crucial aspect of success in any endeavor. It is the foundation upon which success is built at the core of the routine, a sequence of actions or procedures performed regularly. Routine helps to establish patterns of behavior and practice that enable individuals to achieve their goals.

- **Procedure** is an essential element of routine. It refers to the specific steps that must be taken to complete a task or achieve an objective. Procedures help to ensure consistency and accuracy in performance, which is critical for success. For example, in the field of medicine, a specific set of procedures must be followed when performing surgery. Failure to follow these procedures can lead to serious consequences.

- **Practice** is another critical component of routine. It involves repeatedly performing a task or action until it becomes second nature. Practice helps to develop the necessary skills and expertise required to achieve success. For instance, professional athletes must practice consistently to improve their performance and maintain their competitive edge.

- **Patterns** are the final element of routine. It refers to the sequence of actions that are repeated consistently over time. Patterns help to establish habits and behaviors that are conducive to success. For example, a successful entrepreneur may have a routine of waking up early, exercising, and spending several hours working on their business.

- Routine is an essential aspect of Discipline that helps individuals to achieve their goals. It involves using procedures to ensure consistency and accuracy, practice to develop necessary skills, and patterns to establish habits and behaviors that lead to success. By establishing a consistent routine, individuals can build the Discipline to achieve their objectives and reach their full potential.

HOW HAVE I USED ROUTINE AS RELATED TO DISCIPLINE IN MY LIFE:

The "Read the Label" experience vividly highlights the significance of routine in the context of discipline, especially when it pertains to our health and awareness of our surroundings. This incident, where an unexpected encounter with a cannabis-laced product led to an alarming physical reaction, underscores the importance of being vigilant and informed in our daily routines. Just as the discipline of reading labels and being aware of what we consume is crucial for our well-being, this experience serves as a stark reminder of the consequences of deviating from such routines. It emphasizes the need for disciplined adherence to routines that safeguard our health, showcasing how a small oversight can have significant repercussions. This story reinforces the broader principle that maintaining disciplined routines in all aspects of life is key to avoiding unforeseen challenges and ensuring our safety and well-being.

READ THE LABEL

Since my daughters went to college, I have enjoyed being in an empty nest. I spend the winters on Florida's west coast. As I get older, winters are harder for me. As a dedicated golfer, I want to play during all four seasons. People from the east tend to head to Florida for the winters, while those from the west opt for Arizona. Eventually, I will be splitting my time equally between south and the northeast.

During a visit from friends, we enjoyed ourselves, and I introduced them to a local boutique coffee house. I've never consumed coffee, due to my mother's experience of quitting coffee when I was young. An aversion to coffee persisted, and even in Italy, I resisted the allure of espresso. Observing the long lines at airports and coffee chains puzzled me. My friends often go for coffee, and the terminology escapes me.

At this point, why start drinking coffee? I used to consume a lot of sugar but quit years ago. My body may go into shock if exposed to too much caffeine. I occasionally have some green tea, but 99 percent of what I drink is water.

This particular boutique had a great selection of coffee and an array of teas. My friends ordered some coffee concoction, but I opted for jasmine tea and grabbed a chocolate bar from the counter. After enjoying our drinks, we returned to my place. While in a meeting, I noticed a tingling sensation and increasing confusion. The discomfort intensified, affecting my mobility and thoughts. I found myself staring at items in the room.

The feeling intensified. I wasn't numb, but a general sense of cloudiness began to overwhelm me. Paranoia started to be introduced. I found that I could barely walk or contain my thoughts. I was highly uncomfortable. I was not in any pain but in extreme discomfort.

These feelings increased. I called my friends for help, explained my condition, and they checked my vital signs. My blood pressure and heartbeat were all within acceptable parameters. The feelings continued to intensify, making communication difficult and causing extreme discomfort. I found that I could not contain my faculties and that my communication was difficult. What is happening to me? Is this the way I go out? Will this ever stop?

I asked my friends to take me to the emergency room. The next few hours were a bit foggy. As my friends describe, I needed to be led to and from the car by the arm. They handled the paperwork and supported me through this entire process. It was difficult for me to arrange my sentences. I was never belligerent, but very annoyed with what was happening.

Did someone do this to me? Will this ever stop? Is this what it feels like before you die?

All of this was too much for me to handle. Am I going to get better?

I was eventually admitted. I remember being in a wheelchair to the room. I also remember vomiting, and the staff observing and asking, "Do you take drugs? Have you had any alcohol? Have you been drinking water? Has anything been introduced to your body that is unusual? Do you have allergies? Do you take regular medicine?"

I was wheeled to the X-ray room. I was annoyed and confused. I got a CT scan. They had to maneuver me on the machine continually. This took some time. Blood tests were taken. Everything returned within acceptable parameters.

Other tests were performed. I had IVs in both arms. At one point, I remember the doctors saying: this guy is healthier than we are! All of my vitals were fine. My friends were allowed back into the room.

The doctor continued asking me concussion protocol questions:

- Where are you?
- Who is the president?
- What are your friends' names and relationships?
- What is your name?
- What is your children's name?
- How did you get here?

I was able to answer everything. The cloudiness, tingling, and cloudiness would not subside. There was no sense of euphoria at all. What has happened to my body, and would this ever end? I remember the hospital staff hitting on my friends, furthering my annoyance.

After a few hours, they decided to call an ambulance and get me to the large city general hospital where more tests could be conducted because they had reached their limit and could not determine my condition. What was happening?

I remember one of my friends came in and asked, "Joe, do you remember that chocolate bar you picked up at the coffee shop?"

"Yea," I said.

"Well, it had Delta 8 in it. A cannabis-laced treat."

WHAT IS DELTA 8?

Delta-8 is a naturally occurring minor cannabinoid that occurs naturally in cannabis and hemp plants. It is similar in structure to Delta-9 THC, the compound that is responsible for the psychoactive effects of cannabis, but Delta-8 is less potent.

Unlike Delta-9 THC, Delta-8 is associated with distinct effects, including a clearer and more focused high., It is also reported to have fewer adverse side effects like anxiety and paranoia, which some people may experience with Delta-9 THC.

I had limited exposure to cannabis, and it is legal in the state where this occurred. Reflecting on the day's events, my friends and I returned to my place, where I found the wrapper of the consumed product in my office's garbage can. I realized I had unknowingly ingested much more than the recommended dosage –consuming an entire bar of the 24 square pieces. Embarrassed by my oversight, I recalled the doctor's chuckles and declined the offer of an ambulance. I chuckled and said, "I'll sleep this off."

With my friend's help, I returned home and slept off the effects. When I woke up the next morning, I felt 98 percent better, free from any hangover or lingering consequences. I woke up my friends and expressed my surprise that the previous day's events had not resulted in any adverse aftermath.

> *"Discipline is the bridge between goals and accomplishment, and routine is the path that leads us there."*
> —Jim Rohn

DISCIPLINE ELEMENT LESSON LEARNED: ROUTINE

The incident involving a cannabis-laced chocolate bar served as a reminder of the importance of discipline and routine. I learned that even in casual situations, like consuming edibles, adhering to routines and being disciplined can make a significant difference. Neglecting to read the label and consuming the entire bar showed me the value of following routines, like checking labels, to avoid unexpected outcomes. This experience reinforced that discipline and routine go hand in hand, guiding our decisions and actions for better results.

JPDC GUEST: LELAND

Leland views routine as a way to establish Discipline and muscle memory. This empowers him to maintain control and make timely decisions. He believes that routine and Discipline is essential for achieving success, preventing letdowns like lateness or missing significant occasions. Leland values parameters and likes things to be on a schedule but acknowledges that he has had to learn to be more spontaneous in his personal life.

JPDC GUEST: BROOKLYN

Brooklyn sees routine as a way to structure her day and create Discipline in her life. It's about checking the box and continuing daily, even when complicated it involves consistently completing tasks, even amidst challenges. She believes that neglecting necessary actions hinders personal growth. Procrastination is something she tries to avoid because she knows it can lead to lost time and missed opportunities. In summary, Irina sees routine and discipline as essential for personal growth and productivity.

JPDC GUEST: ROCKSON

Rockson views routine as a powerful tool for personal development and self-care. He has crafted a morning routine that serves as a dedicated time for his well-being. Activities like cold plunges, journaling, and reading spiritual literature bring him a sense of balance and positivity. He sees the routine as a foundation for success and approaches the rest of his day with a clear mind and focused intention. Rockson believes that when he focuses on things that connect him to his higher self, he expands his awareness and changes his mindset, making him more resilient and mindful throughout the day. He considers his morning routine a pivotal part of his life and believes that it has a significant impact on his overall well-being.

JPDC GUEST: BETE

Bete views routine as something that provides structure and comfort in her life. She appreciates a systematic lifestyle and credits martial arts for instilling discipline in her routine. Bete believes that having a routine helps prevent emotional distress and mental chaos.

JPDC GUEST: LEILANI

Leilani emphasizes the importance of organization, routine, and Discipline in her life, indicating her strong preference for a structured daily routine. She also highlights the tools she uses to maintain Discipline, such as listening to motivational podcasts and surrounding herself with like-minded people -practices that align with her daily routine.

JPDC GUEST: AUBREY

Aubrey underscores the significance of Discipline and sticking to a routine to achieve personal goals and overcome challenges related to weight loss, perfectionism, and emotional struggles. She also notes that some people struggle with routine and deeper issues related to their past experiences and emotions.

JPDC GUEST: DIEGO

Diego views routine as essential for building a scalable and growing business. He emphasizes the importance of having structures in place to execute repeatedly and consistently over time. Without such structures, businesses may struggle to maintain short-term thinking focused on immediate revenues and sales. Diego illustrates how routines can be difficult to maintain without external accountability, such as having a personal trainer to guide workouts.

7-ORDER

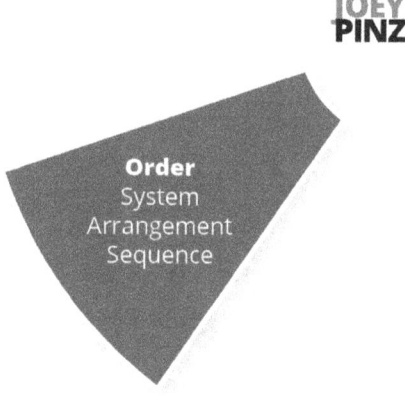

> *Some people regard Discipline as a chore. For me, it is a kind of order that sets me free to fly.*
> —Julie Andrews

We view "Order" as the arrangement or disposition of people or things in relation to each other, according to a particular sequence, pattern, or method. This encompasses the series of steps or actions taken to address an employee's behavior or performance. It also involves a state of obedience or compliance with rules, policies, or procedures that are expected in a workplace, school, military, or other organization. Furthermore, "Order" encompasses the method of teaching or guiding someone to behave in a way that is acceptable or appropriate for their role or situation. This term encompasses concepts like sequence, arrangement, organization, disposition, and structure, referring to how elements are positioned or organized relative to one another. Examples of "Order" include:

- Arranging books on a shelf by genre or author.
- Following a step-by-step recipe to cook a meal.
- Sorting files and documents into folders based on categories.

- Arranging tasks in a to-do list by priority.

Synonyms of "Order" are:
- System
- Arrangement
- Sequence
- Command
- Class

One of the critical components of Discipline is order. Order is the systematic arrangement of things or activities in a particular sequence to achieve a specific objective.

System is an essential aspect of the order. It involves the creation of a framework or structure that guides the arrangement of things or activities in a particular sequence. For example, in a manufacturing plant, a system is put in place to ensure that the production process is carried out in an orderly manner.

Arrangement is another critical element of order. It involves organizing things or activities in a specific pattern or sequence. The arrangement of things or activities determines how efficiently and effectively they can be performed. For instance, the arrangement of tools in a workshop can significantly impact the productivity of a worker.

Sequence is the final element of order. It refers to the specific order in which things or activities are carried out. The sequence determines the process's flow and the activity's outcome. For example, in cooking, the sequence of adding ingredients determines the quality of the final product.

Command in the context of discipline refers to an authoritative order or directive that is to be obeyed. It is a statement expressing a specific instruction or mandate, typically issued by someone in a position of authority. In this sense, a command is an explicit requirement for action or behavior, and it is expected to be followed without question.

Class denotes a level of excellence or quality. In this sense, something or someone that is described as having "class" might be characterized by high standards, excellence, or admirable qualities. This usage implies a disciplined approach to maintaining high standards and often reflects orderliness, respect, and dignified behavior.

In summary, order is an essential component of Discipline that facilitates the achievement of success. By establishing order in our lives, we can become more focused on our goals efficiently and effectively.

HOW HAVE I USED ORDER AS RELATED TO DISCIPLINE IN MY LIFE:

Embarking on the journey of establishing a new business is not only about having a groundbreaking idea or a unique vision; it's fundamentally about embodying the principles of discipline and order. These values are the bedrock upon which successful enterprises are built and sustained. In my own entrepreneurial venture, these principles were not just abstract concepts but daily practices that guided each step of my journey. As I share the story of founding my 'New Corporation,' it becomes evident how discipline, woven intricately with a steadfast commitment to order, was instrumental in navigating the challenges and triumphs of the first year. From the humble beginnings in my father's garage to the significant milestones that marked our growth, every phase of this journey underscores the profound impact of discipline and order in turning a dream into a tangible, thriving business reality.

NEW CORPORATION

Starting a corporation is a challenging feat that requires courage, determination, hard work, and Discipline. This story highlights the challenges faced during the first year of launching a corporation, underscoring the importance of persistence, and not succumbing to setbacks.

In 1993, I initiated my company in my father's garage, engaging in cold calls to potential clients without the luxury of email or the Internet. Cold calling is very humbling. Calling required strategies to get through the "gatekeeper". Some strategies I used were citing connections through personal relationships, golf games, or previous praise.

Through determination and some clever tactics, I was able to gain a few clients. It wasn't easy, but I kept pushing through, attending Chamber of Commerce events, and asking for referrals. Even when the going got tough, I resisted the temptation to burn bridges with former employers. An enduring lesson from this experience is the significance of maintaining professional relationships and avoiding burning bridges, as it can impact one's future prospects.

Eventually, the hard work paid off. We landed two big clients that were game changers for the business. We were even able to bring on a couple of friends to help with the increased workload. This allowed me to gain experience, save money, and have clients as references. As the business grew, I outgrew the garage office and had to find new space. We rented a room from a dentist, which was a significant milestone in the corporation's journey. I made it!

So, to all aspiring entrepreneurs, take inspiration from this story and remember that anything is possible if you have the will to make it happen. Believe in yourself, stay positive, and never give up on your dreams. Who knows, you could be the next success story that inspires others to pursue their dreams.

> *"Discipline and order are the building blocks of success. When we have Discipline, we are able to create order in our lives and achieve our goals."*
> *—Zig Ziglar*

DISCIPLINE ELEMENT LESSON LEARNED: ORDER

On my podcast, 'Joey Pinz Discipline Conversations,' I've had the privilege of hosting a wide array of guests, each bringing their unique life experiences and professional backgrounds. When discussing how discipline plays a pivotal role in their lives, a common theme that emerges is the significant role of order. Each guest, in their own way, has illustrated how maintaining a structured approach to their daily routines, career goals, and personal development is integral to their success and well-being.

JPDC GUEST: RUBY

Ruby views order as necessary for appreciating and understanding the system of government and for making meaningful changes through proper channels. She uses sports as an analogy to explain that rules are important and that one must follow them in order to play the game effectively. She also emphasizes the pivotal role of Discipline, organization, and structure in achieving her goals, especially given the additional time it takes her to complete tasks due to her visual impairment.

JPDC GUEST: AUTUMN

Autumn places a strong emphasis on order and organization within her work. She has methodically structured her floral design business by utilizing her website to streamline operations. She meticulously stores all the necessary event details, including recipes and photos. To maintain a balanced workload and a sense of fulfillment, she intentionally limits the number of one-on-one clients she works with each year. Recognizing the importance of financial clarity, she employs a bookkeeper and accountant to oversee monetary matters and maintain a sense of coherence throughout her business.

JPDC GUEST: AUBREY

Aubrey highlights the importance of order, self-mastery, and self-awareness as crucial factors to understand others and herself. This suggests that establishing a certain level of structure or organization is essential for personal development and cultivating healthy relationships.

JPDC GUEST: ANDRES

Andres views order as a result of commitment and consistency, which are two key components in achieving one's goals. He emphasizes that commitment is essential for starting any goal, while consistency is necessary for maintaining progress and achieving exponential growth. Andres also stresses the importance of planning, as it provides a roadmap to follow and ensures that one's actions are aligned with their purpose. Ultimately, Andres believes that having order in one's life is crucial for successfully pursuing their life's purpose.

JPDC GUEST: ODIN

Odin views order as a means of control and structure, necessary for success in entrepreneurship. He values the freedom of controlling his own destiny but also acknowledges the importance of Discipline and structure. He also expresses a desire to approach education in a more exploratory and creative way rather than enforcing strict rules and regulations. Overall, Odin seems to have a balanced view of order, recognizing its benefits while also seeking to challenge traditional approaches and find new ways of doing things.

8-WILLPOWER

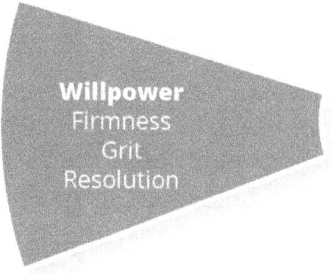

> *"Discipline is the bridge between goals and accomplishment, and willpower is the engine that drives us across."*
> —Zig Ziglar

Willpower is the inner strength and self-control that enables individuals to make intentional choices, resist immediate temptations, and pursue long-term goals. It involves the ability to delay gratification, overcome obstacles, and maintain focus even when faced with challenges or distractions. Willpower plays a crucial role in achieving personal and professional objectives by helping individuals stay committed to their intentions and make decisions aligned with their values and aspirations. Some examples include:

- Resisting the urge to eat unhealthy snacks when trying to maintain a balanced diet.
- Pushing through fatigue to complete a workout or exercise routine.
- Avoiding distractions and staying focused on studying or completing a task.

- Choosing to save money rather than making impulsive purchases.
- Overcoming the temptation to give in to procrastination and tackling tasks promptly.

Some synonyms of willpower are:

- **Self Control**
- **Firmness**:
- **Grit**:
- **Resolution**:

At the core of the Discipline is "Willpower." "Willpower" refers to the inner strength and determination that drives individuals to overcome obstacles and achieve their goals.

Self-control. The ability to regulate one's emotions, thoughts, and behavior in the face of temptations or challenges.

Firmness is an essential aspect of willpower. It involves the ability to remain resolute and steadfast in the face of challenges and adversity. Firm willpower allows individuals to stay focused on their objectives and persevere through difficult times.

Grit is another critical element of willpower. It refers to the resilience and determination that individuals possess in the pursuit of their goals. Grit allows individuals to push through obstacles and setbacks without losing sight of their objectives.

Resolution is the final element of willpower. It involves the unwavering commitment to achieving one's goals, regardless of the obstacles that may arise. A strong resolution enables individuals to maintain their focus and motivation, even when faced with significant challenges.

"Willpower" is a crucial aspect of Discipline that drives individuals to achieve their goals. It involves firmness, grit, and resolution, providing the strength and determination required to overcome obstacles and persevere through difficult times. By developing and cultivating their "Willpower", individuals can become more Disciplined and successful in their endeavors.

HOW HAVE I USED WILLPOWER AS RELATED TO DISCIPLINE IN MY LIFE:

Willpower in discipline is often about channeling one's inner strength to push beyond the apparent limits of possibility. It requires a certain degree of curiosity, a willingness to explore, and a boldness to pursue what seems out of reach. My own 'Superman' story embodies this concept of willpower through an unwavering curiosity and the drive to test the boundaries of what I believed possible.

From the moment humanity left its footprint on the lunar surface, my childhood self was propelled by a dream that seemed as distant as the stars – to become an astronaut. The discipline to acquire knowledge about our celestial neighbors was fueled by a sense of wonder instilled by the historic Apollo 11 mission. My imagination soared with "Star Trek," which opened vistas of space where no man had gone before, and I was right there with them, if only in spirit.

Willpower showed its face not just in the boundless curiosity of my mind but also in the tangible attempts to reach the skies. Emulating Superman, I donned a makeshift cape, believing in the power of flight. That attempt, as ill-fated as it was, didn't deter my spirit. It strengthened my resolve and taught me a profound lesson about the gravity of reality and the discipline required to understand and respect the laws of physics truly. The scar I carry is not just a mark of a childhood misadventure; it's a testament to the willpower that has guided me through life – to dream, to explore, and to rise each time I fall.

SUPERMAN

On July 20, 1969, a historic event took place -the moon landing. From an early age, I held a deep fascination with space and the solar system. The moon landing, in particular, ignited my dream of becoming an astronaut. My fascination drove me to study the planets extensively, even committing their unique traits to memory when

I was just eight years old. Shows like Star Trek captivated me, introducing the concept of space travel and the possibility of other galaxies and species.

My curiosity led me to make an interesting connection between the propulsion systems used in Star Trek and car mufflers. I believed that the Starship Enterprise's powerful nacelle rockets resembled car mufflers and assumed that cars with two mufflers were faster. However, this belief was challenged when I encountered a van with an unconventional muffler placement – it was behind the back tire and on the side in cars. I thought that cars with two fat mufflers were faster than those with only one. This experience taught me the vital lesson that mechanics vary between space and Earth due to gravity and friction. My love for superheroes, especially Superman, inspired me to try flying with a makeshift cape. Unfortunately, my attempt led to a disastrous fall from a second-floor window, resulting in severe injuries and a lasting scar. Instead of opening the window, I jumped through the glass and landed in bushes, resulting in severe injury that required over fifty (50) stitches and left me with a five (5)-inch scar to this day. If we ever meet ask me to show it to you.

These experiences taught me valuable lessons about the importance of researching and understanding the mechanics of things before attempting them. They also showed me that sometimes, what may seem simple in theory can be disastrous in practice.

In conclusion, my early fascination with space and the solar system led me down a path of curiosity and discovery. I learned about propulsion systems and how they work differently in space versus on Earth. I also learned the importance of research and understanding the mechanics of things before attempting them. Though my experiment to fly as Superman ended in a painful lesson, it ultimately taught me valuable lessons that have stayed with me to this day.

> "Discipline is the refining fire by which talent becomes ability, and willpower is the force that turns our desires into reality."
> —Unknow

DISCIPLINE ELEMENT LESSON LEARNED: WILLPOWER

While steadfast in my conclusions, one must have the *willpower* and humility to accept new evidence and accept incorrect perception.

Bridging from the personal to the universal, the theme of willpower resonates deeply in the narratives of my past guests on the Joey Pinz Podcast. Each story is a testament to the incredible power of disciplined resolve. Whether it was an artist turning blank canvases into windows of self-expression despite creative blocks, an entrepreneur relentlessly iterating prototypes to achieve perfection, or a scholar mastering languages to unlock new worlds of knowledge, willpower was the common thread weaving through their diverse journeys.

Their stories illuminate how discipline is not merely a rigid adherence to routine, but an active, dynamic exercise of willpower. It's a conscious choice to pursue a passion, to stay the course in the face of adversity, and to commit to personal growth and excellence. Just as I learned from my 'Superman' experience, they too have embraced the lessons from their trials and errors, allowing their disciplined willpower to guide them to new heights. These conversations have not only shared insights into the successes that discipline can bring but have also highlighted the profound personal transformations that occur when we apply the full measure of our willpower to our endeavors.

JPDC GUEST: ANDRES

Andres views "Willpower" as the key to making choices and stepping outside of one's comfort zone to achieve personal growth and find purpose. He believes that those who take the time to ask and answer hard questions and confront their fears are part of the "fantastic few" who live exceptional lives. He also notes that the brain's natural instinct is to stay in the comfort zone, but willpower allows individuals to overcome this and pursue their goals.

JPDC GUEST: DIEGO

Diego views "Willpower" as a necessary aspect of business ownership, but also recognizes the importance of delegation and allowing others to take on responsibilities. He notes that being a control freak can be limiting, and that it's important to be open to other people doing things differently or even better than oneself. Additionally, Diego acknowledges that some individuals may have a need for control due to their personality or sense of self-worth, and that this may need to be addressed in order to create a more collaborative and effective work environment.

JPDC GUEST: AALIYAH

Aaliyah discusses the "Willpower" concept of "us vs. them" mentality and how easily it can be triggered in human beings. He talks about a study where 9-year-old boys were divided into two groups, and it took only a day before they started hating each other and plotting against each other. Aailyah highlights how this mentality can quickly spiral out of control and result in negative consequences. He also briefly mentions gun control as a topic where people often feel helpless and unable to control the situation. Therefore, it can be inferred that Aaliyah views control as something that can be challenging to achieve in certain situations, particularly when dealing with complex human behavior and societal issues.

JPDC GUEST: GERALT

Geralt views willpower as something that is limited and beyond our power in some respects. He believes that while we cannot control how great our success will be, we do have control over whether we engage in pursuing our goals or not. For him, success is waking up every morning with a mission and clarity, actively putting in effort, and pursuing that mission. He also acknowledges that there will be downtime and unexpected obstacles along the way, but having an intention and a goal to work towards is what defines success for him.

9-DIRECTION

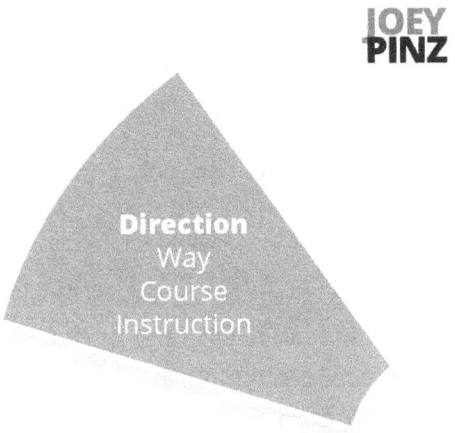

> *The gospel is not a philosophy of repression, as so many regard it. It is a plan of freedom that gives Discipline to appetite and direction to behavior.*
> —Gordon B. Hinckley

"Direction" is understood as a broad concept encompassing the progression of someone or something. It can also signify an authoritative instruction or directive. Rather than a literal indication of a physical path, it denotes the trajectory of a process or journey. Some examples of "Direction" include:

- Career advancement and growth
- Personal development and self-improvement
- Company strategy and objectives
- Educational pursuits and learning goals
- Creative projects and artistic endeavors

Some synonyms are:
- Way
- Course
- Instruction
- Guidance
- Trend

One of the Disciplines' core characteristics is "Direction". "Direction" refers to the path or course individuals must follow to achieve their goals.

Way is an essential aspect of direction. It refers to the route or path individuals must take to reach their objectives. The way involves selecting the appropriate strategies, methods, and tactics to achieve success. For instance, a business owner must choose the right marketing strategies to promote their products or services successfully.

Course is another critical element of direction. It involves the specific steps and actions that individuals must take to reach their objectives. The course includes the establishment of goals, the creation of action plans, and the implementation of strategies to achieve those goals. For example, athletes must follow a specific training regimen to improve their performance and achieve their objectives.

Instruction is the final element of direction. It refers to the guidance and advice that individuals receive to navigate the path to success. Instruction provides individuals with the knowledge, skills, and resources to achieve their goals. For instance, a student must receive proper instruction from teachers to learn and master academic subjects.

Guidance serves as the compass that directs the willpower of an individual towards a purposeful destination. It is the framework within which discipline operates, providing the parameters, knowledge, and wisdom necessary to navigate the often-tumultuous journey towards achieving one's goals. While discipline can be likened to the consistent oars' strokes of a rower, guidance is the rudder that ensures those efforts are steering the boat in the right direction.

Trend is the emergent pattern or practice that gains popularity and becomes influential in shaping behaviors and mindsets. When it comes to discipline, a trend might manifest as a new productivity method, a wellness routine, or even a technological tool that assists in the development and maintenance of disciplined habits.

"Direction" is a crucial component of Discipline that drives individuals to achieve their goals. It involves the way, course, and instruction that provide individuals with the path, steps, and guidance needed to achieve success. By establishing a clear direction, individuals can become more disciplined, and successful in their endeavors.

HOW HAVE I USED DIRECTION AS RELATED TO DISCIPLINE IN MY LIFE:

The trajectory of my college experience serves as a compelling illustration of how a clear sense of direction is integral to the application of discipline. For many, college is a pivotal crossroads, and for me, it was a leap towards not just academic achievement, but also fulfilling a broader vision for my future. The deliberate choice to pursue higher education, despite my parents' ambivalence and the rigor of balancing demanding coursework, was a testament to a disciplined mindset directed towards a specific goal.

The challenges I faced, like completing intensive summer courses and adapting to different learning environments, from a commuter to dormitory life, demanded not just discipline, but also the direction to navigate through them effectively. My decision to engage in side hustles while maintaining academic rigor reflected a disciplined application of entrepreneurial spirit. Moreover, the disciplined pursuit of a computer science degree, despite its gaps in practical training, laid the groundwork for my eventual ventures into the corporate world and entrepreneurship.

This journey from the classrooms of college to the dynamic world of business underscores the power of disciplined direction.

It highlights how a well-charted path, fueled by disciplined effort and adaptability, can open up a spectrum of opportunities. The experience encapsulates the essence of direction within discipline: a guiding force that transforms potential into tangible success.

COLLEGE

Choosing to attend college is a significant and thought-provoking decision for many individuals, and it requires careful consideration. As a son of immigrants, the decision to attend college was not only a personal one but also one that carried familial expectations. My parents were ambivalent about the idea, but I knew it was the right path for me. Although my high school grades were average, my passion for subjects like computers, history, Italian, and physical education set me apart.

My initial college experience wasn't without challenges. To secure admission for the fall semester, I had to complete a summer course in American literature, writing, and another course of my choice. While the computer course was a breeze due to my self-taught knowledge, the writing course presented difficulties. Juggling the demands of crafting two 500-word essays weekly was a huge struggle. I managed to ace the computer course, I earned a C in writing, this experience fueled my determination to pursue higher education. Once I was admitted to college, I found myself commuting for the first year before transitioning to dormitory living. During my time in the dorms, I started some side hustles, including typing and printing term papers for a fee and creating a profitable app for discovering calling card codes. My major in computer science provided me with valuable theoretical knowledge, although practical coding languages used in the professional realm were not fully covered. Graduating in 1992 with a bachelor's degree in computer science, I entered the corporate world, working programming and network support jobs while also serving side clients.

After graduation, I worked some corporate jobs doing programming and network support and also had some side clients I worked for after hours. My experience in college and the corporate world gave me the knowledge and skills to start my own business. My decision to go to college was a wise one, and it opened up opportunities that would not have been available otherwise.

My college demonstrates the role of direction in the realm of discipline, especially in the context of higher education and career growth. Choosing to attend college, despite familial ambivalence and average high school grades, shows a sense of direction driven by personal passion and interest. This decision required a disciplined approach to overcome challenges, such as the mandatory summer courses. While the computer course was in line with the author's skills, the writing course posed difficulties, highlighting the importance of a disciplined focus to improve and balance multiple areas of study. The transition from commuting to dormitory life and the initiation of side hustles are indicative of adaptability and entrepreneurial discipline, channeling one's skills into profitable ventures while balancing academic responsibilities.

The major in computer science offered a directed discipline, equipping the author with theoretical foundations, though not entirely meeting the practical demands of the job market. Nevertheless, the discipline to complete a degree provided the direction that opened doors in the corporate world and eventually led to starting a business. This trajectory exemplifies how discipline, when aligned with a clear sense of direction, can facilitate personal growth and career advancements, underlining the efficacy of making well-considered decisions and following them through with disciplined action.

> *"Discipline is the path to freedom, and direction is the compass that keeps us on that path."*
> —Ryan Holiday

DISCIPLINE ELEMENT LESSON LEARNED: DIRECTION

Reflecting on the diverse tapestry of stories shared by my past podcast guests, the theme of direction emerges as a pivotal aspect of their disciplined lives. Each guest, in their unique narrative, demonstrated the profound impact of setting a clear course and following it with steadfast determination. Just as my college experience was underpinned by the discipline of direction, leading to personal and professional milestones, so too have my guests harnessed this powerful combination to carve out their successes.

JPDC GUEST: BATHSHEBA

Bathsheba views direction as a key ingredient in reaching one's destination, whatever that may be. She emphasizes the importance of being driven and passionate, but also notes that this drive needs to be channeled in a healthy and constructive way. Bathsheba mentions that she has invested a lot of time in personal development to work through emotional trauma and false aspects of herself to get closer to her true self. She also mentions that she is now more structured, organized, and grounded in her approach, underscoring the crucial role of clear direction in attaining success.

JPDC GUEST: MICAH

Micah views "Direction" as an important aspect of business. He suggests that it's important to understand why a partner or customer decides to move in a different direction, and to use that feedback to improve for future partnerships. He also emphasizes the importance of educating and training the sales team so that they have a clear direction and understanding of what they are selling. Overall, Micah views direction as an essential component for success in business and suggests that it's important to stay focused and adaptable to changes in direction.

JPDC GUEST: JOSEPHINE

Josephine regards direction as the compass that aligns with her emotions. She gauges her achievements based on the degree of fulfillment and vitality she experiences. Any feelings of anxiety or stagnation signal to her that she's veering off course. In addition, she highlights the significance of assembling a capable team—a "dream team"—where each member shares the correct trajectory and contributes fresh ideas for the future.

JPDC GUEST: OLIVER

Oliver emphasizes the importance of education for both financial professionals and consumers in the realm of financial planning. He points out that there is a lack of transparency and potential conflicts of interest within the brokerage industry, urging consumers to be informed and seek fee-only financial planners who are unaffected by such conflicts. He envisions fee-only financial planning as the industry's forthcoming direction, one that will elevate financial planning to a true profession.

JPDC GUEST: LEILANI

Leilani underscores the significance of direction in attaining success and fulfilling goals. She stresses the value of immersing oneself in a positive and encouraging environment, engaging with motivational content, and consistently reminding oneself of the objectives to maintain Discipline and concentration. While Leilani recognizes that it can be demanding, she highlights the necessity of depersonalizing it and resolutely committing to staying on course.

10-STRICTNESS

> "Discipline is the bridge between goals and accomplishment, and strictness is the key that unlocks that bridge."
> —Jocko Willink

"**Strictness**" is the quality or condition of being severe. It is one of the key components of Discipline. Strictness refers specifically to the degree of severity, harshness, and rigidity individuals apply to themselves or others to achieve their goals. Some examples of "Strictness" are:

- Imposing rules and regulations for order and control.
- Upholding high standards without compromise.
- Following guidelines and procedures strictly.
- Enforcing discipline and discouraging deviations.

Some synonyms are:
- Severity
- Harshness
- Rigidity
- Stringency
- Austerity

An example of "Strictness" is the quality or state of being demanding or unyielding (as in Discipline or criticism). For instance, a strict teacher might enforce the rules of the classroom with severity and rigor. Another example of strictness is the ability of something to limit someone's freedom. For example, some countries have strict immigration rules that make it hard for people to enter or leave.

Severity is an essential aspect of strictness. It involves the use of stringent measures to enforce rules and regulations. For example, a professor may enforce strict rules in the classroom to ensure that students are attentive and focused on their studies.

Harshness is another element of strictness. It refers to using stern measures to Discipline individuals who fail to adhere to rules and regulations. Harshness can involve punishment or other corrective measures to enforce Discipline patience, a coach may impose a strict training regimen on athletes to improve their performance.

Rigidity is the final element of strictness. It involves the inflexible application of rules and regulations without any exceptions. A rigid approach to Discipline requires individuals to adhere strictly to established standards and procedures. For example, a military organization operates under strict rules and regulations that must be followed without fail.

Stringency refers to the rigorous and strict adherence to rules or standards. It's a quality that involves a level of exactness and inflexibility in following the routines or systems one has set in place. In the realm of discipline, stringency is the backbone of consistency; it's what ensures that one does not deviate from the planned path, regardless of the temptations or distractions that may arise.

Austerity is about the self-imposed practice of simplicity and restraint in pursuit of a greater goal. It is the conscious choice to forego immediate pleasures or indulgences in favor of long-term benefits. Austerity requires a disciplined approach to life, often involving strict budgeting of resources such as time, money, or energy, and it is marked by a deliberate avoidance of excess or luxury.

"Strictness" is a crucial component of Discipline that drives individuals to achieve their goals. It involves severity, harshness, and rigidity, which provide the necessary measures to enforce rules and regulations and maintain Discipline and strictness to themselves or others; individuals can become more disciplined and focused Discipline useful in their endeavors. However, it is essential to balance strictness with compassion, empathy, and understanding to ensure that Discipline is achieved.

HOW HAVE I USED STRICTNESS AS RELATED TO DISCIPLINE IN MY LIFE:

My "Subway Racism" experience from my youth starkly highlights the concept of strictness as it relates to discipline, albeit in a context far removed from the constructive application typically associated with self-discipline. This incident, a jarring encounter with racial prejudice and law enforcement, served as a powerful, albeit distressing, lesson in the harsh realities of societal strictures and their impact.

Strictness, in its most effective and positive form, is about setting and adhering to clear boundaries and standards. However, in this instance, the strictness exhibited by the authorities was not rooted in a fair or justifiable framework but rather in prejudice and a misuse of power. It underscored how strictness, when applied without fairness or understanding, can lead to negative and lasting consequences.

This experience, while deeply unsettling, also offered a crucial lesson in empathy and the importance of discerning right from wrong within the structures of authority and societal rules. It was a stark reminder that while discipline and strictness are vital in shaping character and guiding actions, they must always be tempered with justice and humanity. This incident not only shaped my understanding of the world but also reinforced my commitment to a disciplined life that respects and upholds the dignity of all individuals.

SUBWAY RACISM

Growing up, many of us have experiences that shape our perspectives and understanding of the world around us. Spending time with cousins in New York City as a teenager provided me with both positive and negative experiences that have stayed with me. One experience that stands out, in particular, is getting my first fake identification in Times Square. This ID allowed me access to clubs and alcohol but only worked about half the time.

Times Square in the 80s was full of porn, fake ID shops, shell games, drugs, and prostitutes. However, in present times, it has become a tourist destination, and locals are nowhere to be found.

My friends and I were teenage boys listening to hip-hop artists like RUN DMC, The Beastie Boys, Public Enemy, and LL Cool J. They would jump turnstiles on the subway to avoid paying and head into the city to explore. However, a traumatic event occurred during one of my visits that would have a lasting impact. My cousin left early, leaving seven African American friends and me behind. They decided to leave the city and jump turnstiles to avoid paying for the subway. This was not an uncommon occurrence for them, and they had managed to avoid getting caught in the past.

This time would be different. The station was at a dead end, with no trains to jump on. We were caught.

The officers were not in a good mood this particular night. They put us against the wall. They started saying racial things to my friends. When a particular cop approached me, he asked me why I would be friends with these *racial slur*.

Absolutely horrifying.

This lasted for what felt like hours but probably was only 15 minutes. They made calls and eventually let us go. The train ride back was silent. I felt horrible and guilty, even though I didn't do anything wrong. Our friendship suffered after this terrible event.

This experience illustrates the consequences of lax discipline and the impact of a strict authoritative environment on individual choices and societal attitudes. As teenagers exploring Times Square in the 1980s—a locale infamous for its lack of regulations and oversight—we seemed emboldened to engage in activities such as using fake IDs and jumping turnstiles, behaviors symptomatic of a lack of personal discipline. However, this lack of discipline meets a harsh reality when the group encounters law enforcement officers who exercise strictness in a discriminative and abusive manner. The traumatic event serves as a wakeup call, forcing a reevaluation of the risks associated with indiscipline and the grave consequences that can come from a rigidly enforced yet flawed system. This story encapsulates the complexities of strictness in relation to discipline, showing that while a lack of discipline can lead to negative outcomes, strictness that is untampered by fairness and humanity can be equally damaging.

> *"Discipline is the foundation of all achievement, and strictness is the rule that ensures that foundation is solid."*
> *—Unknow*

DISCIPLINE ELEMENT LESSON LEARNED: STRICTNESS

Reflecting on the narratives shared by my past podcast guests, the role of strictness within the framework of discipline emerges as a defining factor in their paths to success. Much like the harsh but instructive lessons from my "Subway Racism" experience, these individuals have harnessed strictness in a constructive manner, channeling it to create boundaries, maintain focus, and achieve remarkable feats in their respective fields.

Their stories reveal how applying strictness, not as a means of constriction but as a tool for focused growth, has enabled them to excel. From entrepreneurs who imposed stringent schedules on themselves to maximize productivity, to artists who set non-negotiable standards for their creative output, each guest demonstrated a disciplined adherence to their own rigorously set rules. This strictness, much like the lessons learned from my own experiences, was not about rigidity for its own sake, but about creating a disciplined environment where goals could be pursued with unwavering dedication and precision.

In each conversation, it became evident that strictness in discipline is a powerful ally when it's aligned with clear goals and ethical considerations. It's a balance of maintaining high standards while navigating the complexities of life, much as I learned in navigating the complexities of societal structures and personal ethics from my youth. These guests exemplify that when used wisely and judiciously, strictness in discipline can be a key ingredient in crafting a successful and fulfilling life.

JPDC GUEST: SAVANNAH

Savannah's perspective on strictness centers around how bullies often use it to boost their self-esteem and manage their own insecurities. She points out that bullies tend to exert control over others and surround themselves with followers to elevate their sense of worth. To counteract this, she advises young individuals to refrain from engaging with hurtful online comments, enabling them to maintain emotional control and avoid being hurt. In addition, Savannah recommends parents inquire about classroom dynamics and popular figures among their kids, fostering a deeper understanding of the situation and aiding in the prevention of bullying.

JPDC GUEST: LEILANI

In Leilani's perspective, strictness used to be synonymous with the wealth she possessed in the past. Yet, she came to a profound realization that the abundance of money did not bring her true contentment. Nowadays, she directs her focus towards finding fulfillment through her relationships with individuals. Leilani places importance on surrounding herself with those who share her outlook, as they become a crucial support system for her aspirations. This inclination hints at her appreciation for the influence she wields over her surroundings and the company she elects to keep.

JPDC GUEST: SOPHIE

In Sophie's perspective, the notion of strictness extends its influence across diverse facets of existence, encompassing domains such as finances and sexuality. She observes that the compulsion to manage one aspect often translates into a compulsion to manage the other. Sophie further posits that nurturing one's sexual energy can generate a magnetic and formidable aura, potentially fostering a sense of control. She delves into the topic of how societal norms often result in young women embracing birth control and contraception, possibly severing their connection with innate intuition and their potent capabilities. On the whole, Sophie's outlook conveys that control possesses both constructive and detrimental potentialities, interwoven with various spheres of life.

JPDC GUEST: MICAH

Micah underscores the significance of maintaining a sense of strictness to attain objectives and uphold productivity. He highlights the adoption of tools like monday.com as a means to enhance organization and concentration. Micah also proposes that exercising control over elements such as workout schedules, reading habits, and dietary choices can streamline the process of adhering to disciplined routines.

JPDC GUEST: JOSEPHINE

Josephine views strictness as it mainly discusses the topic of founder syndrome and how Walt Disney was able to let go of control and bring in the right people to take the company to the next level.

DISCIPLINE SPECTRUM ASSESSMENT

A Discipline Spectrum assessment is gathering and evaluating information about a situation, hobby, skill, or experience related to Discipline. The assessment can help you identify discipline strengths while providing valuable feedback on improving your learning and/or performance.

An assessment can help you set realistic, achievable goals and measure your progress. It can demonstrate your understanding of a subject matter and show your competence and readiness for further challenges. It can help you gain insight into your personality, interests, values, or motivations and guide you toward suitable choices or opportunities.

The first step is to Define the subject of the assessment.

The subject of an assessment is the topic or situation being evaluated or measured. For example, Golf, losing weight, and/or trying to get a raise at work are all topics and/or situations that could use assessment. Some more examples may be:

- Cooking
- Martial Arts
- Accounting
- Pickleball
- Gardening
- Essay Writing
- Public Speaking
- Leadership

Here is a sample worksheet assessment:

DISCIPLINE IS A SPECTRUM

	Subject:	Score 1 (Strongly Disagree) to 5 (Strongly Agree)
1	Focus (Center, Concentrate, Emphasize)	
2	Restraint (Unemotional, moderation, limitation)	
3	Obedience (Compliance, Dutifulness, Submissiveness)	
4	Mastery (Proficiency, Skill, Expertise)	
5	Control (Influence, Authority, Power)	
6	Routine (Procedure, Practice, Pattern)	
7	Order (System, Arrangement, Sequence)	
8	Willpower (Firmness, Grit, Resolution)	
9	Direction (Way, Course, Instruction)	
10	Strictness (Severity, Harshness, Rigidity)	
	Total:	

To get the full worksheet assessment, go to www.joeypinz.com/SpectrumAsessment

Now, it's your turn. Make your personalized list of subjects you'd like assessed. Rank each characteristic by a score of 1 to 5. Once completed, total the rankings. This is the score. The perfect score is 50, and the weakest score is 10.

While your answers are entirely subjective, try your best to be honest with yourself.

The Discipline Spectrum Assessment is an assessment that measures how people use real life situations. Discipline includes many principles limited to the ability to follow the rules, create order, and maintain consistency. People with a strong Discipline theme enjoy routine and prefer to plan ahead and stick to their schedules.

The Discipline Spectrum Assessment can be used for various purposes, such as:

- Identifying one's own strengths and weaknesses in Discipline.
- Developing and increasing one's self-Discipline skills and habits.
- Comparing one's Discipline style with others to discover new and improved methods.
- Enhancing teamwork and collaboration by understanding different Discipline preferences
- Improving performance and productivity by applying Discipline strategies

SUMMARY

The Discipline Spectrum Assessment provides valuable insights into one's own or others' Discipline. It can also help identify areas for improvement or development. Using the Discipline Spectrum can teach how to use discipline effectively in different situations.

Example: Tiger Woods

I remember being on a golf range and making pure contact with the ball. I was hooked. It felt so good. I started taking golf lessons and even purchased my first set. I bought my first set of inexpensive knockoffs, cheap clubs. Golf is often considered a solitary sport, where you primarily play on your own, even if you are part of a group. Keeping your own score adds to the individual nature of the game.

One of the unique aspects of golf is that there is no one else to blame but yourself when playing. On the flip side, there is also no one else to credit but yourself when you perform well. However, little did I anticipate the lengthy duration of a round of golf and the associated costs.

Fortunately, I have the opportunity to share the love of golf with my close friends. We often travel together and engage in various activities centered around the game.

Playing eighteen holes of golf with someone provides valuable insights into their character. For example, you can observe whether they are prone to anger and resort to throwing clubs when things don't go their way. Their level of engagement and passion for the game becomes apparent, as you can determine if they truly care about their performance or display apathy. You can also gauge their appreciation for the course architecture and the intricacies of each hole. Some individuals may showcase a strong interest in golf equipment, displaying a fascination with the gear they use. Additionally, golf often attracts individuals who enjoy gambling, turning the game into an opportunity for friendly wagers and competition. Observing their behavior regarding alcohol consumption during the game can reveal whether they choose to drink and how it affects their performance.

When it comes to business relationships, playing golf with clients can significantly deepen the connection. It provides an opportunity to spend quality time together, and it is common to follow the game with a meal and a celebration, further strengthening the professional bond.

Becoming skilled at golf requires taking lessons and maintaining dedication and Discipline. It is a sport that humbles even the most talented athletes from team sports who mistakenly believe they can transition effortlessly. While the golf swing involves athleticism, swinging harder or faster, often leads to less productive results.

As an experienced golfer, I often discourage newbies from taking up golf. I don't want them to blame me when they miss a putt or complain that it takes too long or is too expensive. I want them to take it seriously if they want to play.

When it comes to giving golf swing tips, I refrain from doing so. With my current five-index handicap, I have always received instruction from dedicated and knowledgeable professionals. I respect their dedication and expertise, and I understand that what works for me may not work for others. Besides, my swing mechanics are tailored to my low-ball trajectory. Therefore, I always suggest contacting a local certified golf training professional and take lessons. You won't regret it.

Tiger Woods, with his numerous tournament wins, played a significant role in golf's popularity peak. He serves as a true inspiration to many within the sport.

Tiger Woods is the most famous and successful golfer of all time. He was born in California to an African American father and a Thai mother. He started playing golf at a very young age and became a prodigy, winning many amateur tournaments and appearing on TV shows.

Woods turned professional in 1996 and quickly dominated the sport with his powerful swing, precise shots, and competitive spirit. He won his first major championship, the Masters, in 1997 by a record margin of 12 strokes. He went on to win 14 more majors, including four Masters titles, three U.S. Open titles, three British Open titles, and four PGA Championship titles. He also won 82 PGA Tour events (tied for first with Sam Snead), achieved the world number-one ranking for a record 683 weeks (including a streak of 281 weeks), and earned more than $120 million in prize money.

Woods faced many challenges and controversies in his career, such as injuries and surgeries. He also had periods of poor performance and loss of confidence. However, he always managed to overcome adversity and make remarkable comebacks. His most memorable comeback was winning the Master's for the fifth time in 2019 after undergoing four back surgeries.

Woods is widely regarded as one of the greatest golfers ever and one of the most influential athletes in modern history. He has inspired millions of people worldwide with his talent, passion, Discipline, determination, and resilience.

DISCIPLINE IS A SPECTRUM

I devote a significant amount of time to practicing golf, playing numerous rounds throughout the year, and participating in various tournaments. Achieving excellence and maintaining consistency in golf requires unwavering dedication and Discipline. Golf has the potential to serve as a metaphor for life.

In golf, we abide by the principle of "play the ball as it lies." Once the ball lands, we can't pick it up and move it to a more favorable place. This concept is similar to the saying "you made your bed; you lie in it."

When you swing at the ball in golf, you are completely on your own. There is no one else to hold responsible but yourself. The execution of the swing solely depends on your abilities and actions.

In golf, no two shots are the same. The sport presents numerous variables and factors to consider. Being an outdoor game, there are various obstacles to contend with. The wind, moisture on the ball or landing surfaces, and environmental conditions like humidity or dryness all influence the game. Moreover, the ball's flight can be affected by factors such as temperature. Additionally, the line of the ball on the grass can vary, including scenarios where it may be on even ground, in a divot, below or above your feet, uphill, or downhill. Furthermore, the conditions of the green come into play, including its hardness or softness, the position of the pin (whether its short, long, left, or right), the shapes and slopes of the green, and the presence of sand bunkers near the green. Understanding where to miss and where not to miss also becomes crucial. In essence, golf encompasses a multitude of factors that continuously challenge players on every shot. This makes you adapt to your surroundings and variables to calculate your club selection and approach to the next shot.

Risk & Reward –In golf, there is a constant evaluation of risk and reward. Should you attempt to target a pin that's positioned in a precarious spot? If you miss slightly to the left, it may result in a challenging recovery. Alternatively, aiming your drive to the right may involve some danger, but it can potentially lead to a better setup for the next shot.

Similar to life, taking chances becomes necessary. The level of success achieved depends on weighing the odds and making calculated decisions.

Golf serves as a meaningful metaphor for life, sharing valuable lessons and parallels with our daily experiences. Here are some ways in which golf resembles life.

1. Patience and Perseverance: Golf requires Dedication and practice to master its skills, just as life demands patience and perseverance to overcome challenges and achieve personal growth.
2. Adaptation and improvisation: Similar to how golfers must adjust to changing conditions like weather and terrain, life presents us with unpredictable circumstances that necessitate adaptability and create problem-solving.
3. Learning from mistakes: Golf provides opportunities to learn from errors and setbacks, reminding us that life is a journey of growth and self-improvement where mistakes can be valuable lessons.
4. Enjoying the moment: Beyond its competitive aspect, golf offers moments of relaxation, camaraderie, and simple enjoyment. Similarly, life offers experiences beyond work or achievement, emphasizing the importance of finding joy and connection.

Golf can be more than just a sport; it can also be a way of living, offering enduring passion and the opportunity for participation even in old age. The game of golf mirrors the ups downs, challenges and joys that we encounter throughout our lives.

The game of golf replicates life in many ways.

I have a strong passion for golf. I can hopefully do it way into the elderly years of my life.

DISCIPLINE ASSESSMENT – BECOMING A SCRATCH GOLFER:

The subject is not just playing golf but specifically becoming a scratch golfer.

A scratch golfer is a player who has a handicap of zero or below, which means that they can play at or better than par on any rated golf course. Par is the number of strokes a skilled golfer should need to complete a hole or a course. A handicap is a numerical measure of a golfer's potential ability based on their past performance.

A scratch golfer is considered very good at golf, as they can hit accurate shots, make tricky putts, and avoid mistakes. They have consistent skills and strategies that allow them to play well on different courses and conditions. Only about 2 percent of golfers are estimated to be scratch golfers.

To become a scratch golfer, one must practice regularly, improve swing mechanics, learn course management, develop mental toughness, and play with other skilled players. It takes dedication, Discipline, and passion to achieve that level of golfing excellence.

	Subject: Become Scratch Golfer	Score 1 (Strongly Disagree) to 5 (Strongly Agree)
1	Focus (Center, Concentrate, Emphasize)	3
2	Restraint (Unemotional, moderation, limitation)	1
3	Obedience (Compliance, Dutifulness, Submissiveness)	1
4	Mastery (Proficiency, Skill, Expertise)	4
5	Control (Influence, Authority, Power)	3
6	Routine (Procedure, Practice, Pattern)	5
7	Order (System, Arrangement, Sequence)	2
8	Willpower (Firmness, Grit, Resolution)	2
9	Direction (Way, Course, Instruction)	5
10	Strictness (Severity, Harshness, Rigidity)	2
	Total:	28

The assessment is purely subjective. We give a total of 28. What do you give?

To get the full worksheet assessment, go to www.joeypinz.com/book.

CHAPTER 3

5 STEPS TO SUCCESS AND HAPPINESS

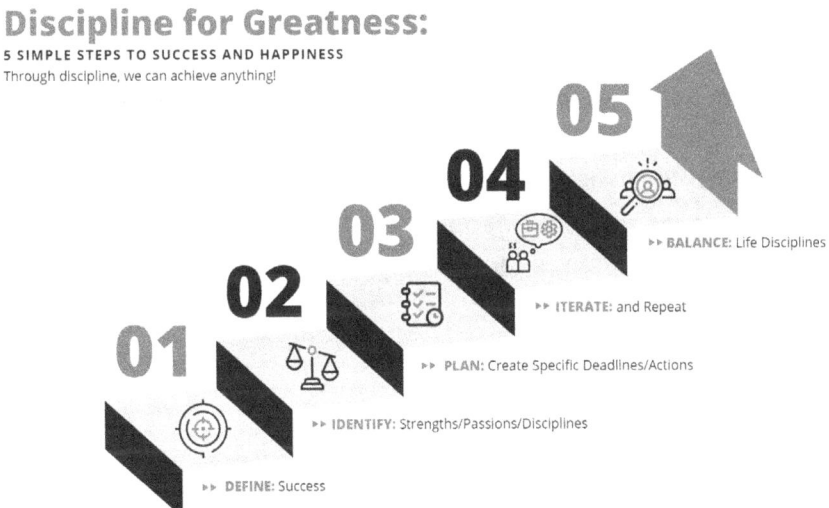

Now that we have explored the four *Life Disciplines, what* do we do with it?

There are five simple steps to success and happiness. To excel, you need to be able to answer the hard questions. With Discipline, you can work at these steps.

STEP ONE: DEFINE WHAT *PERSONAL SUCCESS* MEANS TO YOU.

> "Success is liking yourself, liking what you do, and liking how you do it."
> —Maya Angelou

Defining what success is to you is the start, and perhaps, the most crucial step. From your definition, the process to success becomes clearer. Continuously revisiting and refining this definition ensures ongoing progress.

Personal success can mean different things to different people. For some, success may be defined by the accumulation of wealth or material possessions. For others, success may be measured by achievements, accomplishments, and personal growth.

Alternatively, personal success may mean living a fulfilling and purposeful life that aligns with their values, goals, and aspirations. It may involve pursuing happiness, contentment, and inner peace, rather than the accumulation of external markers of success.

STEP TWO: IDENTIFY YOUR *STRENGTHS AND PASSIONS* AND USE THEM TO PURSUE YOUR GOALS.

Understanding your capabilities, strengths, and areas for improvement is vital for personal development. What are you good at? What are your strengths and weaknesses? How many of the characteristics of the Discipline spectrum do you possess? Which do you need help with?

Identifying your strengths and passions is a crucial step toward achieving your goals. When you know what you're good at and love doing, you can channel your efforts and energy toward fulfilling and rewarding pursuits.

Strengths refer to your natural abilities and talents that you possess. Identifying your strengths can help you determine what you're good at and what you enjoy doing. It can also help you build confidence and self-esteem as you recognize your unique skills and abilities.

Passions refer to your interests and things that you enjoy doing, without external incentives. Rewarding your passions can help you find purpose and meaning in your life as you engage in activities that align with your values and bring you joy.

Once you have identified your strengths and passions, you can use them to pursue your goals. By aligning your goals with your strengths and passions, you can create a clear and compelling vision of what you want to achieve and leverage your natural talents and interests to pursue them.

For example, if you're passionate about strength training and fitness, you can use your passion to motivate and inspire others to achieve their fitness goals. Similarly, if you're good at writing and passionate about social justice, you can use your writing skills to create content that raises awareness about social issues and inspires people to act.

Identifying your strengths and passions can help you pursue your goals with greater clarity, purpose, and motivation. By leveraging your natural talents and interests, you can create a fulfilling and rewarding life that aligns with your values and brings you joy. So, take the time to explore your strengths and passions and use them to create a meaningful, purposeful, and fulfilling life.

STEP THREE: CREATE A *PLAN WITH SPECIFIC ACTIONS AND DEADLINES.*

An NFL coach once famously stated, "If you fail to plan, you plan to fail." One needs to create a plan to achieve success and happiness. For some, this is the most challenging task. Specificity is key—actions must be defined with set deadlines, ensuring accountability and progress.

Why is it so imperative to create a plan with specific actions and deadlines?

Creating a plan with specific actions and deadlines is essential for several reasons.

First, the plan prioritizes tasks and activities. It provides a strong and clear roadmap of what needs to be accomplished and when, individuals can allocate their time and effort effectively, concentrating on pivotal tasks while sidestepping distractions.

Second, a plan with specific actions and deadlines provides much-needed structure and directions. It furnishes individuals with a clear idea of what needs to be done and how to achieve it. This can help to reduce stress and anxiety, as you have a roadmap to follow and a sense of control over your tasks and responsibilities.

Third, adherence to a plan heightens the likelihood of goal attainment. By breaking down goals into actionable steps and imposing deadlines, you can create a sense of urgency and momentum toward achieving your goals by breaking down your goals into specific, actionable steps and setting deadlines for each step. This can help you stay motivated and committed and progress towards your goals even when faced with challenges or setbacks.

Lastly, a meticulously crafted plan with specific actions and deadlines can help you track your progress and adjust as needed. By regularly reviewing your plan and assessing your progress, you can identify areas where you need to make changes or adjustments and make course corrections to keep you on track toward achieving your goals.

Creating a plan with specific actions and deadlines is essential for providing structure and direction, prioritizing tasks and activities, increasing the likelihood of achieving your goals, and tracking your progress. So, take the time to create a specific, actionable, and deadline-driven plan as a roadmap toward achieving your goals.

STEP FOUR: IMPROVE AND REPEAT.

Improvement and repetition play pivotal roles in the development of personal plans, enabling individuals to refine and enhance their strategies over time. Continuously reassessing and revising the plan ensures its relevance, achievability, and alignment with goals and values. Goals that need to be adjusted may be achieved sooner or later. Ask others for feedback and learn from your mistakes.

Here is a breakdown of the key steps in the process:

1. The first step in iterating and repeating is to review the plan and assess progress toward goals regularly. This can help to identify areas where they need to make changes or adjustments, and to refine the plan accordingly. For example, if not progressing towards a particular goal, one may need to adjust the timeline, change the approach, or seek additional support or resources.
2. Gather feedback from others, such as friends, family, or mentors. This can provide valuable insights and perspectives that can help to identify blind spots, overcome challenges, and make improvements to the plan. For example, if you're struggling to balance your work and personal life, a mentor or coach may be able to provide guidance and support to help you better manage time and priorities.
3. Be flexible, adaptable, and embrace change as a natural part of the process. As you work towards goals, you may encounter unexpected challenges or opportunities, and priorities or values may shift over time. One can adjust the plan to stay aligned with goals and values by remaining open and flexible.

Ultimately, it's essential to recognize that creating a personal plan is an ongoing process requiring consistent effort and commitment. Regularly iterating and repeating can continually refine and improve the plan and stay on track toward achieving goals.

Iterating and repeating are essential aspects of creating a personal plan. They allow one to refine and improve the plan over time, gather feedback from others, be flexible and adaptable, and recognize that creating a personal plan is an ongoing process. It's necessary to take the time to regularly review and revise the plan, seek feedback and support from others, and stay committed to the goals and values over the long term.

STEP FIVE: BALANCE YOUR WORK AND PERSONAL LIFE.

Achieving balance across personal, family, professional, and community aspects of life demands a significant amount of discipline. It requires conscious decision-making regarding which areas need focused attention at various intervals, whether it's hourly, daily, weekly, monthly, quarterly, semi-annually, or annually.

Balancing work and personal life are vital for well-being, success, and happiness. It can be challenging to juggle the demands of all four life Disciplines, personal, family, professional, and community. Still, with a few simple strategies, it is possible to achieve a healthy balance.

Here's a breakdown of effective strategies to balance these life disciplines:

- Establish clear boundaries. This means establishing specific work hours, sticking to them, and carving out time for personal activities and relationships. By setting clear boundaries, you can reduce stress, improve productivity, and make time for the things that matter most to you.
- Prioritize self-care. This means taking care of physical, mental, and emotional well-being, such as exercising, eating healthy, getting enough sleep, engaging in activities to track your progress, and prioritizing self-care. One can recharge batteries and better manage the demands of life Disciplines.
- Utilize technology and tools to your advantage. This means using apps, calendars, and other tools to manage time, stay organized, and reduce time spent on mundane or repetitive tasks. Technology and tools can improve efficiency and effectiveness and make time for the things that matter most.
- Communicate effectively with all of life's Disciplines. This means being honest and transparent about needs and priorities and setting realistic expectations for oneself and others. Communicating effectively can reduce stress and misunder-

standings and foster positive relationships and collaborations.

Balancing life's Disciplines of personal, family, professional, and community spheres is essential for overall well-being and happiness. By setting clear boundaries, prioritizing self-care, communicating effectively, and using technology, track your progress, adjust a healthy balance, and make time for the things that matter most. Consider taking the time to assess your current life balance and make the necessary adjustments to achieve a better long-term balance.

Let's dive deep into the five steps!

STEP 01 DEFINE SUCCESS

▶▶ **DEFINE:**
Success

> Success is not final; failure is not fatal: it is the courage to continue that count.
> —Winston Churchill

What does it mean to be successful? How do you measure your success? These are some of the questions many people ask themselves about their life and career. Success is not a one-size-fits-all concept. It is a personal and subjective experience that depends on your values, goals, dreams, and aspirations.

Perhaps success is when you reach your aim or purpose. It is when you achieve what you set out to do, big or small. Success is when you feel happy, fulfilled, and proud of yourself and your accomplishments. It can also be when you live the life you always wanted and have no regrets. But how do you define success for yourself? How do you know what your aim or purpose is? How do you set your goals and dreams?

Here are some steps that can help you:

Focus on Yourself: Don't compare yourself to others or follow social norms or expectations. Success may not be about money, fame, power, or popularity; it's about being true to yourself and living authentically. Only you can decide what success means to you.

Reflect on Accomplishments: Think about what you have done so far in your life and career that makes you feel successful. What skills did you use? What challenges did you overcome? What impact did you make? These can give clues about what matters to you and motivate you.

Think Large and Small: Success can be achieved at different levels and areas of your life. You can have personal, family, professional, and community success. You can also have short-term goals, long, long-term, and daily goals.

Think about what kind of success you want to achieve at each level and area. Defining a specific personal success is an exciting journey that allows you to discover yourself, your potential, and your purpose. It empowers you to take charge of your life and pursue your passions. It inspires you to grow as an individual and contribute positively to society.

Remember, success is not a destination but a journey. It is not something that happens overnight but requires constant effort and improvement. It is not something others can give you but something you can only create for yourself. So go ahead and define your success!

You have the power, the potential, and the passion! You are awesome! You are successful! I ask all of my guests on the podcast how they define success. I received various answers.

Many at first say that it's not financial. But when one says it's not something, on the offset, one must wonder if there is an element of half-truth. There is nothing wrong with financial success. Many seek absolute independence as the pinnacle of achievement.

One must ask what will be done once financial independence is achieved. You can't be too rich or too skinny. Many have heard this.

Is it true? Is financial success the goal or just being rich? Rich is an ambiguous term. What is rich for one may not be for another.

Wealth is another level, often when large sums of money are inherited or are generations old. If money is your definition of success, we need to dive deeper as that question encourages a deeper understanding of one's values and priorities in the pursuit of a fulfilling and meaningful life. But, first, *what will you do with the money?*

WHAT WILL YOU DO WITH THE MONEY?

DONATIONS

Financial success opens avenues to allow you to help others. Here is an example: A soccer player who plays in Europe refuses to fly private and spends generously to help his African village, which includes giving each citizen a monthly stipend. He introduced internet access, built hospitals, and transformed schools. Beyond these soccer players' acts, there are other global organizations that could use financial aid to help national issues such as water cleanliness, war, education, sexism, racism, abuse, and trauma.

INVEST

Some view financial success as an opportunity to improve society. They choose to invest in ways that foster growth among the recipients of their investment. This includes supporting corporations which can help employees and economies. Additionally, investing in nonprofits, for example, can have helpful global benefits.

HEALTHCARE

In the face of sickness and disease, money allows people to live longer for themselves, their families, and others. The ability to afford healthcare not only benefits individuals but also impacts their families and communities. However, it is important to acknowledge that healthcare expenses can vary significantly depending on the nature of the medical issue.

TRAVEL

While travel is often considered a valuable form of education, it can be financially demanding. Despite the cost, some aspire to explore the world, gaining different experiences and perspectives.

MAKE PARENTS PROUD

Another answer I hear to the question of what to do with success is a desire to make parents proud. Parental affirmation plays a pivotal role in a person's lifelong journey. Positive feedback from parents is a critical component of a child's emotional and psychological development. When parents offer positive feedback and show appreciation for their children's efforts, it instills confidence and self-worth in them. On the other hand, when parents are critical or dismissive, it can adversely affect a child's self-esteem and confidence. Parental affirmation should be balanced with constructive feedback to support ongoing growth and development.

Financial success presents various opportunities to positively impact individuals, communities, and society at large. Whether through philanthropy, investment, healthcare, access, travel experiences, or familial validation, the uses of financial success are diverse and multi-faceted.

DIFFERENT WAYS TO DEFINE *SUCCESS* DEPEND ON ONE'S GOALS AND VALUES.

In the pursuit of success, individuals interpret success differently. Some standard definitions of success are:

- A favorable or desired outcome.
- The accomplishment of an aim or purpose.
- The attainment of wealth, favor, or eminence.

- The achievement of a desired goal.
- A performance or achievement that is marked by success.

DEFINING SUCCESS IN THE LIFE DISCIPLINES

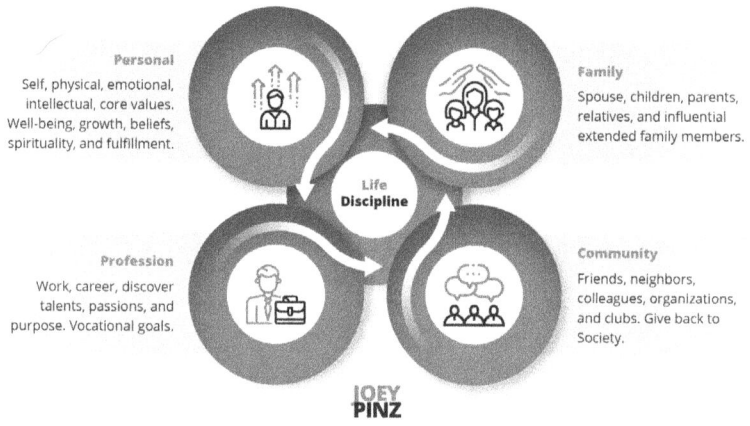

> Success is not the key to happiness. Happiness is the key to success. If you love what you are doing, you will be successful.
> —Albert Schweitzer

Success in your Personal Discipline necessitates grappling with challenging questions that encompass various aspects of self: physical, emotional, intellectual, core values.

Considerations regarding health and well-being are paramount. Obesity is a national epidemic. Currently, in the USA, obese and overweight people are over 75 percent. Should success be healthy? As for me, this was a significant barrier. When the doctor told me I would not see my daughter graduate, that was all I needed to hear. It was my "come to Jesus" moment.

A *come to Jesus*' moment is a phrase that has two possible meanings. One meaning is when people accept Jesus Christ as their savior and follow the Christian faith. Another meaning is when a person suddenly realizes or recognizes they need to change their behavior or attitude. For example, someone might have a *come to Jesus'* moment after being fired for laziness.

Have you suffered from trauma? If so, what are you doing about it? Trauma is a significant issue in our world. Traumatic experiences, often overlooked in youth, can manifest later in life, necessitating varied approaches to healing, including counseling, medical care, and medication.

I have been fortunate to interview many from trauma. They have all dealt with it differently. Many need co-counseling medical care and medication.

SPIRITUALITY

Many view spirituality as a large portion of their personal Discipline. Reflecting on where you are in your spiritual journal and assessing fulfillment levels can shed light on areas for further exploration and development.

Furthermore, establishing and adhering to personal core values is integral to navigating life's complexities and making ethical decisions. Do you have personal core values? Have you gone through the exercise of creating personal core values and holding to them? When you have core values, many decisions are made much more straightforwardly, facilitating clarity and consistency in decision-making processes. Whenever a difficult decision presents itself, one must refer to their core values to conclude.

Personal core values encompass your foundational beliefs, which then dictate your behavior and guide your decisions. They are essential because they help you align your actions with your purpose and goals. They also help you communicate better with others and build trust and respect.

Some examples of personal core values are honesty, kindness, loyalty, integrity, compassion, and creativity.

FAMILY DISCIPLINE

Family

Spouse, children, parents, relatives, and influential extended family members.

> Success is not measured by what you accomplish, but by the opposition you have encountered, and the courage with which you have maintained the struggle against overwhelming odds.
> —Orison Swett Marden

How do you define success in your family Discipline? Are you the best husband, wife, father, mother, uncle, aunt, cousin, grandfather, grandmother, son, or daughter you can be? Often family gets put on the back burner, and it gets taken for granted. For those in the family that needs contact, are you communicating with them enough? Some family members may have said they need less contact. Are you complying?

Do you have a routine with the family that aids in a cohesive family unit? Are you striking a balance between being present for your family and fulfilling work obligations? Are you providing adequate support without becoming overly intrusive in your children's lives?

Success within the Family Discipline encompasses the happiness, health, and well-being of individual members, as well as the quality of interactions with the family unit.

The individual members' characteristics include their happiness, health, and well-being. The characteristics of the family interaction, such as their communication, support, and harmony. The extent to which the family fulfills certain functions, such as raising children who establish stable families themselves. Reflecting on these aspects can guide you in assessing and enhancing your family's overall success and fulfillment.

PROFESSION DISCIPLINE

Profession

Work, career, discover talents, passions, and purpose. Vocational goals.

> Success is to be measured not so much by the position that one has reached in life as by the obstacles which he has overcome.
> —Booker T. Washington

Many individuals prioritized their careers to maintain their lifestyle, recognizing the crucial role a career plays in providing purpose, financial security, skill development, social connections, and societal identity.

Defining success in professional Discipline can be subjective and varies from person to person. Success in a profession can be measured in different ways, including personal satisfaction, financial stability, and recognition from peer recognition.

Personal satisfaction is a crucial aspect of success in any profession. It means feeling content and fulfilled with work and accomplishments. Having a passion for your job and feeling a sense of purpose in what you do may be essential. If you wake up excited about going to work every day and feel a sense of fulfillment at the end of each day, you may be on the path to success.

Financial stability is also a significant factor in determining success in any profession. A stable income provides security and allows you to enjoy a comfortable lifestyle. It means meeting your financial obligations and investing in your future.

Peer recognition is also an essential aspect of success. It means being respected by colleagues and being recognized for contributions. This recognition could come through promotions, awards, or conference speaking engagements. Being recognized by your peers indicates that you have significantly impacted your profession and earned respect and admiration from those around you.

Success in the professional Discipline combines personal satisfaction, financial stability, and peer recognition. Setting goals and striving towards achieving them while maintaining a passion for your work is essential. Success cannot be achieved overnight, but it is a journey that requires dedication and hard work.

How do you define success in your professional Discipline?

COMMUNITY DISCIPLINE

Community

Friends, neighbors, colleagues, organizations, and clubs. Give back to Society.

> Success is not about being the best. It's about always getting better.
> —Behance founder Scott Belsky

The final aspect of Life Discipline is community. Defining success in a community can be challenging as it involves many factors that inspire the community's overall well-being. Success in a community can be measured in different ways, including social cohesion, economic growth, environmental sustainability, and civic engagement.

Social cohesion is the strength of the social bonds between individuals in a community. Success in a community may be achieved by fostering a sense of community spirit, where individuals work together towards common goals, support each other during difficult times, and celebrate each other's achievements.

Environmental sustainability is another significant factor in defining success in a community. A sustainable community is mindful of its impact on the environment, adopts environmentally friendly practices, and encourages residents to adopt sustainable habits. This can include promoting recycling, reducing carbon emissions, and preserving natural resources.

Economic growth is another crucial factor in determining the success of a community. A thriving economy creates job opportunities, attracts investments, and stimulates local businesses. When a community has a strong economy, it can provide its residents with access to a high standard of living and opportunities for personal and professional growth.

Another essential component is civic engagement in a community. When residents actively participate in community decision-making processes, it promotes transparency, accountability, and inclusivity. It creates a sense of ownership and empowerment among community members, resulting in a more cohesive and resilient community.

Defining success in a community involves a complex chemistry of social, economic, environmental, and civic factors. Success can be achieved by fostering a sense of community spirit, promoting economic growth, adopting sustainable practices, and encouraging civic engagement. Ultimately, success in a community is achieved when its residents are happy, healthy, and thriving.

HOW DO THE GUESTS ON THE JOEY PINZ PODCAST DEFINE SUCCESS?

JPDC GUEST: BATHSHEBA

Considers success to be having a great personal brand that seems to associate success with self-belief and giving value to others.

JPDC GUEST: BETE

Describes success as achieving their goals and feeling good about themselves. For Bete, success means feeling empowered, beautiful, and sexy by dressing to impress and viewing things differently in the office by wearing business attire. looking professional and confident in their work environment.

JPDC GUEST: ROCKSON

Believes success means being able to get curious about themselves, ask questions, work with the answers, and make changes based on those answers. They also mention having support around them and releasing pain as part of their definition of success.

JPDC GUEST: ANTHONY

Views success through the lens of opening up the conversation between Muslims and Americans and reducing the ignorance and misconceptions on both sides. They also imply that success would involve a more accurate portrayal of Islam in the media and a more objective understanding of what's happening worldwide.

JPDC GUEST: SOPHIE

Measures success by being able to speak about her sexual partnerships and relationships openly and embodying her sexuality in her business. She also seems to value respect and empowerment for sexually promiscuous women.

JPDC GUEST: MICAH

Success in digital marketing can mean different things to different organizations, but some common ways of measuring it are:

- User engagement: how users interact with your online content and channels
- Conversion funnel: how users move from awareness to action (such as purchase, sign-up, etc.)
- Brand perception: how users view your organization's identity and reputation
- Internal collaboration: how well your team works together to achieve digital marketing goals.
- Customer service processes: how you handle user feedback and complaints
- SMART goals: specific, measurable, achievable, relevant, and time-bound objectives for your digital marketing efforts
- Digital marketing as being online, creating content, building a following and running paid ads. They also mention organic reach and engagement as important factors.

JPDC GUEST: JOSEPHINE

Finds success in having a clear vision of where they want to go, a mission of how they will get there, and a purpose of why they exist. They also imply that success involves getting people involved and aligned with their vision.

JPDC GUEST: GABRIEL

Thinks of success as achieving one's goals and desires in life and career rather than following conventional formulas or standards of success. They also imply that success requires more than hard work, such as competency, planning, and creativity. Success is also personal and may change over time.

JPDC GUEST: VALENTINA

Equates success with achieving health and wellness using nutritional science and therapy. They also mention how nutrition affects their mind and how they experience life.

JPDC GUEST: OLIVER

Interprets success as the attainment of wealth, favor, or eminence, as well as the accomplishment of one's goals. They also imply that success involves helping people with investing and financial planning and being a fiduciary means putting their client's interests ahead of their own.

JPDC GUEST: SAVANNAH

In her eyes, success looks like the accomplishment of an aim or purpose, such as overcoming bullying, growing a thick skin, working as an executive, and handling difficult customers. They also imply that success involves hard work, resilience, and self-confidence.

JPDC GUEST: AUTUMN

To her, success means business as balancing multiple responsibilities and goals, such as family, work, and personal growth. They also value Discipline, mindset, and passion as individual drivers of success. They view success as a process rather than a destination, and they have specific examples of achievements.

JPDC GUEST: LEILANI

When asked, she said success is overcoming childhood abuse, trauma, and alcoholism, and finding a sense of self and survival.

JPDC GUEST: AUBREY

Sees success as achieving self-mastery and knowing oneself through a combination of science, art, and nonverbal experiences. They also imply that success involves finding a balance between being self-obsessed and being unaware of oneself.

JPDC GUEST: ANDRES

Considers success to be solving a social problem with a business perspective and generating a profit that can be used for social impact. They also mention some examples of social entrepreneurs such as Tom's shoes. A social entrepreneur is someone who establishes an enterprise with the aim of solving social problems or affecting social change.

JPDC GUEST: AXTON

Describes success as being aggressively curious, hurdling obstacles, figuring things out, focusing on solutions, and pushing for innovation. He also implies that success requires hard work and planning.

JPDC GUEST: BROOKLYN

Believes success means being persistent and sticking with an idea until it works. She also implies that success requires understanding the customer and changing the perspective when selling software.

JPDC GUEST: DIEGO

Views success through the lens of:
- The accomplishment of an aim or purpose.
- The attainment of wealth, favor, or eminence.
- The ability to innovate, deliver change, and improve communities.

JPDC GUEST: LELAND

Measures success by being able to control as much as you want in the music industry and not complaining about the flaws of the system. He also implies that success is related to monetizing your music through streaming platforms. Success in the music industry can be defined differently depending on your goals, skills, and values. Some possible ways to define success are:

- Having a loyal fan base that supports your music and engages with you.
- Making a living from your music through various income streams.
- Creating music that expresses your artistic vision and satisfies your creative needs.
- Collaborating with other musicians or producers that inspire you and challenge you.
- Reaching a wider audience through exposure on media platforms or live performances.
- Having a positive impact on society or culture through your music.
- Receiving recognition or awards from peers or industry professionals.

JPDC GUEST: RUBY

Finds success in making it work with what they have and being grateful for the opportunity to do what they love. They also attribute their success to their faith and God's healing. They don't focus on the challenges or difficulties of being legally blind but rather on the practice and experience they have gained over their lifetime.

JPDC GUEST: ODIN

Thinks of success as accomplishing an aim or purpose, such as giving a keynote speech at a legal tech conference or doing a TEDx talk. They also mention some indicators of success, such as fame, wealth, social status, or being good at solo sports.

JPDC GUEST: GERALT

Equates success with making their way in tech for 45 years and not feeling like a victim despite the unfairness and discrimination they faced. They also imply that fairness is what you make of it, meaning success depends on how you perceive and respond to your situation.

JPDC GUEST: AUDREY

Interprets success as being able to experience and understand the culture and the people of the place they visit. They also mention that success depends on how much preparation and time they have before and during their travel. They imply that success is not just about visiting a place but also learning from it and building layers of understanding.

JPDC GUEST: CLAIRE

Interprets success is working hard for something, putting in many hours, and learning new things. She also mentions that being an entrepreneur is exciting for us because it's something new and there's so much to learn.

JPDC GUEST: WESTON

Sees success as achieving their goals, helping their clients, and providing value to their business. They also mention some factors that can contribute to success, such as experience, heart, and planning.

JPDC GUEST: DELILAH

Considers success to be being curious and learning new things. They both have different perspectives on what makes them happy and fulfilled.

JPDC GUEST: AALIYAH

Describes success as resolving conflict and diffusing tension by listening profoundly and detecting lies. She believes that all conflict starts with tension and that most people are not listening but rehearsing what they want to say.

JPDC GUEST: KINSLEY

Equates success with growing from discomfort, embracing difficulties, accessing humanity, and building trust with clients.

SUMMARY

Before achieving success and happiness, describe what success means to you. Only you can answer what success looks like. This is the beginning of our journey to success and happiness.

STEP 02 IDENTIFY: STRENGTHS, PASSIONS, AND DISCIPLINES

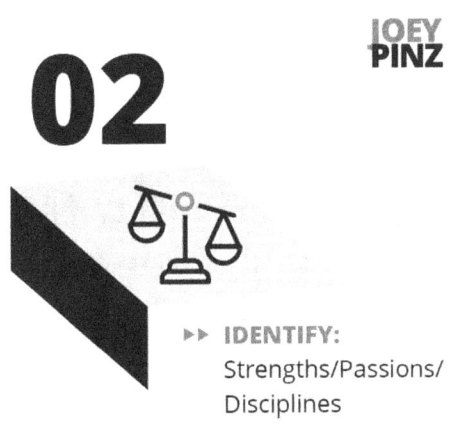

▶▶ **IDENTIFY:**
Strengths/Passions/Disciplines

> When you identify your strengths, you can leverage them. When you identify your weaknesses, you can improve them. But when you identify your passions, you can bring out the best in yourself.
> —T. Harv Eker

Once we define success, we need to understand ourselves better. Identify your strengths and passions and use them to pursue your goals.

Do you know what your personal strengths are?

Do you know what makes you unique, talented, and valuable?

Do you know how to use your strengths to achieve your goals and live a fulfilling life? If not, don't worry. You are not alone. Many struggle with identifying and leveraging their personal strengths.

But it doesn't have to be that way. You can discover your strengths and unleash your potential with some simple steps.

Personal strengths are the attributes, activities, or tasks that you outshine in. They are skills and abilities, personality traits, cognitive abilities, and character traits. They make you stand out from the crowd and give you an edge over others. They can also make you content, confident, and motivated.

But how do you find your personal strengths?

How do you know what they are and how to use them?

HERE ARE SOME WAYS THAT CAN HELP YOU:

Take a strengths test: One of the easiest ways to identify your personal strengths is to take a test that measures them. Many online tests can assess your strengths based on scientific research and evidence. We have created a test to determine your strengths based on the ten elements of the Discipline spectrum. Visit www.joeypinz.com/book.

Talk with your family, relatives, friends, and coworkers: Another way to find your personal strengths is to ask for feedback from people who know you well. Your family members, friends, colleagues, or mentors can give you valuable insights into what they think are your best qualities and abilities. You can also write down what they say and look for patterns or themes.

Identify and acknowledge your weaknesses: Knowing your weaknesses can help you find your strengths. By being honest about what you struggle with or need to improve on, you can focus on what you do well or enjoy doing instead. You can also use your weaknesses as opportunities to learn new skills or seek help from others with complementary strengths.

Find where you are productive: Another clue to finding your strengths is looking at where you are most productive and efficient. Think about when you feel engaged and enthusiastic about your work or activities. What tasks or projects do you complete with ease, speed, and quality? What skills or talents do you use in those situations? These can indicate your personal strengths.

Understand your passions: Your passions can also reveal your personal strengths. Think about what interests you, what excites you, what inspires you, and what drives you. What topics or issues do you care about deeply? What causes do you support wholeheartedly? What activities or hobbies do you love doing for fun? These can show your personal strengths.

Leave your comfort zone: Sometimes, your personal strengths may be hidden or dormant because you have not tried new things or challenged yourself enough. Going outside your comfort zone allows you to discover new aspects of yourself and unlock new potential. You can try new experiences, learn new skills, meet new people, and explore new opportunities. You may surprise yourself with what you can do.

Create a support network: Finding your personal strengths is not something you have to do alone. You can create a support network of people who encourage, support, and celebrate you. You can seek guidance from mentors, coaches, or counselors who can help you identify and develop your personal strengths. You can also join communities of like-minded people who share your passions, values, and goals. You can learn from them, collaborate, and inspire them with your strengths.

Finding your personal strengths is an exciting process that helps you know yourself better, value yourself more, and live more authentically. It empowers you to pursue your goals and dreams with confidence and determination. Your unique gifts and talents enable you to contribute positively to society. Everyone has personal strengths that make them unique, extraordinary, and successful. So go ahead and find yours! You have the power, the potential, and the passion!

PERSONAL STRENGTH TESTS

Personal Strength Tests are tools designed to measure your personality traits or characteristics that make you unique and valuable. There are different types of personal strength tests, such as:

1. **Clifton Strengths assessment.** This test involves answering questions about how you think, feel, and behave.
2. **Myers-Briggs Personality Type Indicator (MBTI).** This test identifies your preferences across four dimensions of personality: extraversion/introversion, sensing/intuition, thinking/feeling, and judging/perceiving.
3. DISC Personality Assessment focuses on behavioral traits categorized into Dominance, Influence, Steadiness, and Conscientiousness. It's best for: Communication styles, team roles, leadership training.

We have created a great free strength test on www.joeypinz.com/StrengthTest

THE DISCIPLINE SPECTRUM STRENGTH TEST

Now that you've been introduced to the ten core elements of discipline, it's time to reflect: which of these strengths are already guiding your life—and which ones need your attention?

The Discipline Spectrum Strength Test is designed to measure your personal strength in each of these ten traits. It's not abstract. It's practical. In just a few minutes, you'll generate a detailed picture of your current discipline profile.

Each of the ten questions in the test corresponds to one of the ten elements you've just explored. You'll score yourself from 1 (strongly disagree) to 5 (strongly agree), based on how well each statement reflects your behavior and mindset.

This self-assessment isn't about perfection. It's about awareness—recognizing where you are strong, where you are developing, and where a focused effort could transform your results.

HERE'S WHAT THE JOEY PINZ STRENGTH TEST WILL MEASURE:

Focus – Your ability to direct your attention. Are you able to concentrate on what matters without getting pulled off course? This score reveals how well you protect your attention in a distracted world.

Restraint – The strength to pause before reacting. Restraint is about holding back impulsive decisions and operating from intentionality. This score shows how well you self-regulate in the heat of the moment.

Obedience – Your relationship with structure and authority. Not blind compliance, but your ability to follow proven systems, routines, and external accountability when it supports your mission.

Mastery – The pursuit of skill over time. This score reflects how committed you are to learning, practicing, and refining what you do—not just dabbling, but striving for excellence.

Control – Your ability to maintain emotional and behavioral stability. Do you keep your composure when things go sideways? This score highlights how much internal authority you truly have.

Routine – The daily patterns that build your life. This element measures how consistent and reliable your habits are—whether you can create structure and stick to it.

Order – The level of clarity and organization in your world. This score reflects how well you manage your time, environment, and responsibilities to reduce chaos and increase focus.

Willpower – Your ability to do hard things, especially when they're not exciting. This score shows whether you can sustain action when motivation fades.

Direction – How clearly you've defined your path. Discipline without direction can become empty effort. This score measures the strength of your personal mission and how well your actions align with it.

Strictness – The standard you hold yourself to. This is about personal boundaries and non-negotiables—the internal expectations that define how you show up.

Once you complete the test, you'll receive a score for each element, along with a total score that places you within one of four profile categories. These categories aren't meant to label you—they're designed to help you see exactly where you are on your discipline journey.

Whether your results show that you're just getting started or already demonstrating high-level consistency, this insight will give you clarity. You'll know what's working. You'll know what to reinforce. And you'll know where to go next.

You can take the test for free at www.joeypinz.com/book. It's fast, insightful, and built to give you a baseline for building your personal discipline plan.

JOEY PINZ DISCIPLINE PODCAST GUEST STRENGTHS.

While the guests of the podcast did not necessarily take the strength test, based on our conversation, we may infer these strengths:

JPDC GUEST: BATHSHEBA

Concepts and the importance of being authentic in one's personal branding. She also emphasizes the significance of self-belief and comfort with one's natural state.

JPDC GUEST: ROCKSON

His strengths include articulating his thoughts and ideas clearly and effectively. He can also use personal experiences to provide insight into mental health issues and the importance of vulnerability. Additionally, he can empathize with others and understand the different struggles that different people face and the societal expectations that contribute to those struggles.

JPDC GUEST: ANTHONY

His strengths include his ability to explain complex issues in an easy-to-understand manner, his extensive knowledge and understanding of Islam and the Western world, his ability to provide objective information and verifiable facts, and his willingness to engage in open and honest conversations about challenging topics. He also seems skilled at connecting historical events and ideas to current issues and problems and recognizing and addressing misconceptions and misunderstandings about Islam.

JPDC GUEST: SOPHIE

Their strengths include her advocacy for women and her belief in the power of embodying sexuality in business. She also has sales experience and believes she has a superpower in reading people and asking challenging questions due to her perceived softer approach as a woman. Additionally, she has a strong sense of self-worth and does not let slut shaming affect her.

JPDC GUEST: MICAH

Their strengths include his knowledge and expertise in digital marketing, particularly in search engine optimization (SEO) and paid advertising. He emphasizes the importance of having an online presence and building a following through organic reach and engagement. Hemant can provide examples of businesses successfully utilizing digital marketing strategies, including doctors in rural areas targeting potential patients through Geo-targeted paid ads. He is also knowledgeable about the pros and cons of SEO and advertising and can provide insight that can linger effectively together. Additionally, Hemant stays current with industry changes and trends, such as the iOS change affecting e-commerce businesses.

JPDC GUEST: JOSEPHINE

Is strong in:

- Strengths can be inferred from her response to the question about the importance of vision in a business.

- She demonstrates a strong understanding of the critical role of a clear vision in achieving results and getting people to follow you.
- She also shows the ability to communicate complex ideas in a simple and relatable way, using a metaphor of a car trip to explain the importance of having a vision. Additionally, she mentions the three categories that organizations use, showing a deep understanding of organizational strategy and structure.
- Her strengths can be summarized as strategic thinking, communication skills, and expertise in organizational development.

JPDC GUEST: GABRIEL

Shows strength in:

- He is a professional basketball player who went from his high school bench to a 9-year career in just five years.
- He is a pioneer in mental game mastery, helping entrepreneurs and athletes dominate their game from the inside out.
- He has given many TEDx Talks and authored 33 books on Discipline, confidence, mental toughness, and personal initiative.
- He has appeared in national campaigns with Nike, Finish Line, Wendy's, Gatorade, Buick, Wilson Sports, STASH Investments, and TIME magazine.

JPDC GUEST: VALENTINA

Strengths as a nutritional therapist are:

- She clearly and concisely defines what a nutritional therapist does, which helps explain her role and expertise to potential clients or collaborators.

- She emphasizes the holistic and individualized approach of nutritional therapy, which shows that she is attentive to the needs and preferences of each person she works with.
- She demonstrates her knowledge and passion for nutrition and its effects on health and wellness, which can inspire trust and confidence in her services.
- She shares her personal story and background to connect with her audience and show how she became interested in nutrition and hormones, which can make her more relatable and authentic.

JPDC GUEST: OLIVER

Strengths as a financial advisor are:

- He has a good reputation and invokes confidence and trust by being a fee-only financial planner and a fiduciary.
- He takes a proactive approach by explaining his title and what he does for his clients.
- He is an experienced financial professional who knows the difference between wealth management and financial advising.
- He takes a holistic view of his client's finances by helping them with investing and financial planning.

JPDC GUEST: SAVANNAH

Their key strengths include:

- She is charismatic, highly energetic and entertaining.
- She is a nationally recognized, award-winning educator who provides teachers, parents, and administrators with the tools and confidence they need to create a culture of civility throughout school communities.
- She is a former fashion and retail executive who taught fashion marketing and career exploration/personal finance classes.

- She is an actor who has performed in shows.
- She is a sprinter who competes in senior games and holds state records for the 50 and 100 meters.

JPDC GUEST: AUTUMN

Notable strengths are:

- She is multitasking and can handle multiple responsibilities at once.
- She has a strong motivation to succeed for her kids.
- She is resourceful and can work with what she has.
- She has a growth mindset and is unsatisfied with the status quo.
- She has the Discipline and time management skills to juggle all the things and prioritize the right things.

JPDC GUEST: LEILANI

Leilani brings strength in:

- She has a prevailing sense of self and survival.
- She has been able to tell her story with clarity and honesty.
- She has sought therapy to heal from her past wounds.
- She has not let the negative opinions of others define her.

JPDC GUEST: AUBREY

Is strong in:

- She has a clear introduction and a hook that engages the listener's interest and curiosity.
- She demonstrates her expertise and credibility by mentioning her academic background, teaching experience and coaching practice.
- She uses examples and anecdotes to illustrate her points and make them more relatable.
- She shows enthusiasm and passion for her topic and conveys a positive tone throughout her speech.

JPDC GUEST: ANDRES

Strengths as a social entrepreneur are:

- He has a clear definition of what a social entrepreneur is.
- He can identify a problem that he wants to solve from a business perspective but with a social impact attached to it.
- He can explain the difference between a nonprofit and a social venture.
- He is willing to take on the risk and effort to create positive social changes through his initiatives.

JPDC GUEST: AXTON

Strengths that Tim has are:

- Curiosity: He describes himself as "aggressively curious" and says entrepreneurs always push for innovation and see solutions.
- Resilience: He mentions that entrepreneurs must overcome obstacles and cope with ups and downs.
- Realism: He advises people to exercise caution in their planning and not be swayed by the glorified word of an entrepreneur.

JPDC GUEST: BROOKLYN

Shows strength in:

- She speaks clearly and coherently without repeating or contradicting herself.
- She uses relevant vocabulary and grammar for the topic and context.
- She expresses her opinion confidently and convincingly, using words like "I believe" and "it requires".
- She listens actively to the interviewer, nodding and saying "yes" or "um" to show interest and understanding.

JPDC GUEST: DIEGO

Demonstrates strength in:

- speaks fluently and confidently, without hesitations or pauses.
- uses appropriate vocabulary and grammar for the topic and context.
- expresses her opinions clearly and supports them with examples and facts.
- engages with the interviewer by asking questions and showing interest.
- uses body language and tone of voice to convey enthusiasm and emotion.

JPDC GUEST: LELAND

Notable strengths are:

- He is a podcast veteran with much knowledge and insight about the music industry.
- He is optimistic and realistic about the opportunities and challenges for independent artists.
- He is confident and articulates in expressing his opinions and arguments.
- He is passionate and enthusiastic about music and creativity.

JPDC GUEST: RUBY

Is strong in:

- She is a successful author despite her visual impairment.
- She has a positive and resilient attitude toward her challenges.
- She has a strong faith and belief in God's healing power.
- She has a lot of experience and practices coping with her condition.

JPDC GUEST: ODIN

Shows strength in:

- Running: He says he was always really good at running, and he sounds confident about it.
- Tennis: He mentions tennis as one of the solo sports he was good at, and he seems to enjoy it.
- Skiing: He also mentions skiing as a solo sport he excelled at and sounds happy about it.
- Storytelling: He says that working with a coach to learn how to tell stories was as fun or even more fun than doing the TEDx talk. He also speaks with enthusiasm and detail about his experience.

JPDC GUEST: AALIYAH

Demonstrates strength in:

- She is an expert in mediation and conflict resolution, with over 30 years of experience and a reputation for crafting creative and pragmatic solutions.
- She is keen to manage big egos and strong personalities and create synergy among diverse groups.
- She has a deep understanding of human communication, emotions, and motivations and can detect when someone is lying or hiding something.
- She can engage her audience with exciting metaphors, examples, and stories illustrating her points.
- She is confident, assertive, charismatic, respectful, empathetic, and humble.

JPDC GUEST: GERALT

Geralt has a strong sense of self and does not feel like a victim of discrimination. He is confident and resilient in his career. He has robust solutions to why tech has not been fair to minorities and women.

JPDC GUEST: AUDREY

Strengths might be:

- She has a good command of English and can express herself clearly and fluently.
- She has much travel experience and can share her insights and perspectives on different cultures and places.
- She is respectful and curious about other people's cultures and tries to learn from them.
- She is adaptable and flexible when things go wrong or unexpectedly during her travels.

JPDC GUEST: HUNTER

Strengths are:

- He has a deep understanding of the anatomy and physiology of the human body and how yoga affects it
- He has a unique perspective on why stretching can be harmful and how to practice yoga safely and effectively.
- He has a sense of humor and can make his listeners laugh with his jokes and anecdotes.
- He is passionate about yoga and sharing his knowledge and experience with others.

JPDC GUEST: CLAIRE

Strengths as an entrepreneur are:

- She is motivated to achieve and is willing to work hard for her goals.
- She has a nonconformity and is not afraid to try something new and different from her previous career as a soccer player.
- She has a passion for her business and enjoys learning about being an entrepreneur.
- She has teamwork skills and can collaborate effectively, as she learned from playing soccer.

- She has a street-smart ability and can deal with practical problems and challenges in her business environment.
- These are some of the typical qualities of successful entrepreneurs that Claire seems to demonstrate in her transcript. Of course, other aspects of her performance may not be captured by this short sample.

JPDC GUEST: WESTON

Strengths as an attorney are:

- He is passionate about his job and wants to help small to medium business owners with their legal needs.
- He has compassion for his clients and does not try to sell them unnecessary services.
- He has excellent communication skills and can explain complex legal concepts in simple terms.
- He has good research skills and can provide valuable client resources, such as the strongly protected business checklist.
- He has creativity and can tailor his legal advice to different situations and stages of business growth.
- These are some of the typical traits of successful attorneys that Weston seems to demonstrate in his transcript. Of course, other aspects of his performance may not be captured by this short sample.

JPDC GUEST: DELILAH

Some strengths are:

- She is curious and well-read, which can make her more knowledgeable and engaging.
- She has a unique perspective and personality, which can make her stand out from other podcasters.
- She can connect with her audience by being honest and authentic about herself and her opinions.

JPDC GUEST: KINSLEY

As a speaker who gave a TEDx talk about embracing the difficulties and challenges in life and work, they are also a non-binary, sober, world-record-holding strongman competitor and published author specializing in cultivating mental toughness.

Some of their strengths are:

- They are confident and assertive about their identity and pronouns.
- They are knowledgeable and passionate about their topic of interest.
- They can connect with the audience by using examples and anecdotes from their experience.
- They are resilient and persistent in overcoming obstacles and achieving their goals.

STEP 03 PLAN: CREATE SPECIFIC DEADLINES AND ACTIONS.

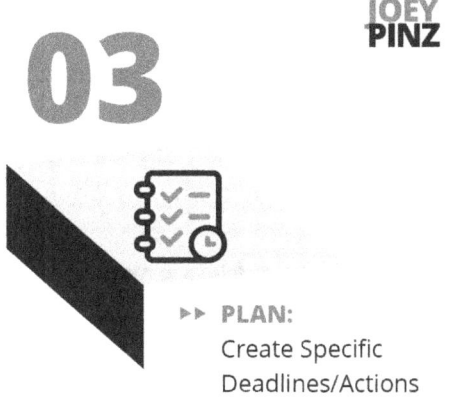

▶▶ **PLAN:**
Create Specific Deadlines/Actions

> A good plan executed today is better than a perfect plan executed next week.
> —General George S. Patton

Creating a personal plan involves setting goals and objectives for your personal development and determining the actions you need to take to achieve them.

Do you have a personal success plan? Do you know what you want to achieve and how to get there? Do you have a clear vision of your goals and a strategy to reach them? If not, don't worry. You are not alone. Many people don't have a personal success plan that works. But it doesn't have to be that way. You can create your success plan with some simple steps.

A personal success plan is a roadmap that guides you toward your desired outcomes. It helps you identify your strengths, weaknesses, opportunities, and challenges. It helps you set realistic and measurable goals and track your progress. It helps you overcome obstacles and stay motivated. It helps you grow personally and professionally.

But how do you create a personal success plan that works? How do you ensure it aligns with your values, passions, and purpose? Here are some ways that can help you:

1. **Evaluate your current situation and define your goals**: Assess where you are and want to be. Identify what's working well in your life and what isn't, along with your strengths and areas you are happy and unhappy about. Note areas where you need to improve.
2. **Determine your goals**: Define what you want to achieve in life, both short-term and long-term. Consider personal, family, professional, and community goals, aligning them with your values, passions, and purposes.
3. **Recognize the obstacles and challenges**: Identify internal and external factors that may impede your progress, as well as potential risks and uncertainties. Develop strategies to overcome, avoid, or minimize these obstacles or challenges.
4. **Create an Action Plan**: Outline specific steps and tasks needed to achieve your goals, along with the necessary skills, resources, and support. Establish deadlines, milestones, and indicators of success to track your progress effectively.
5. **Execute your plan and monitor results**: Implement your action plan, regularly reviewing your performance and adjusting your actions as needed. Celebrate achievements and reward yourself along the way to stay motivated.

By following these steps, you can embark on an exciting journey of personal growth, achieving your goals and realizing your dreams. This empowers you to pursue what truly matters with confidence, determination, and resilience, fostering continuous learning, improvement, and innovation in all aspects of your life. It enables you to grow personally with your family, professionally, and in your community with continuous learning, improvement, and innovation. Remember, everyone has the potential for greatness.

5 STAGE PERSONAL PLAN

5-Stage Personal Plan:

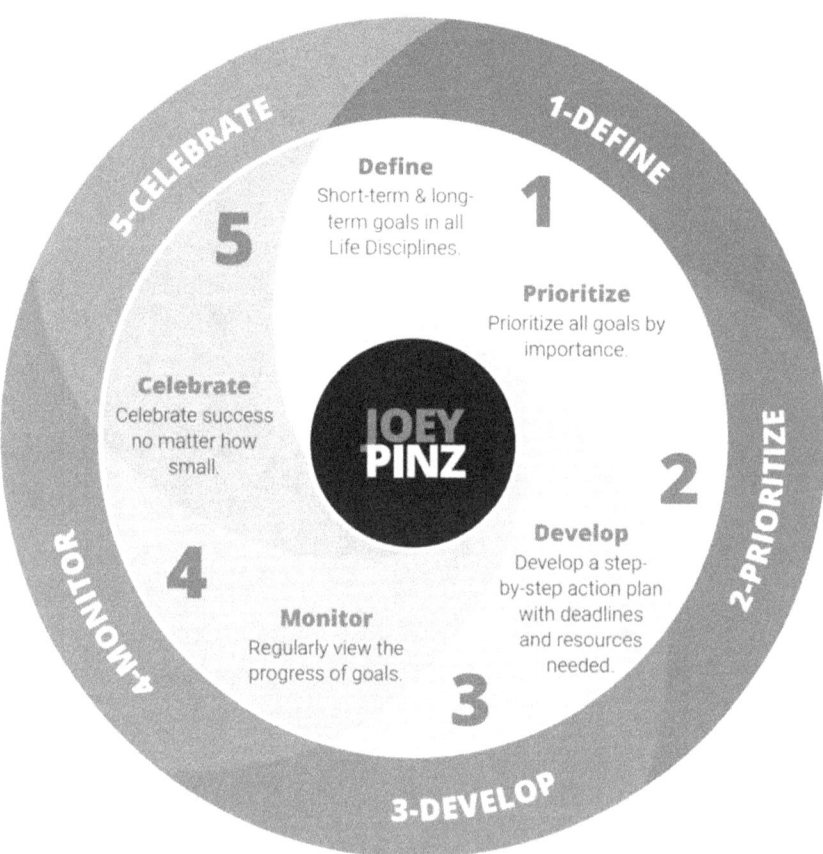

Creating a plan is the third step in the five simple steps to success and happiness.

This is the stage where we commit our goals to paper. Writing the goals adds another level of commitment.

1-DEFINE

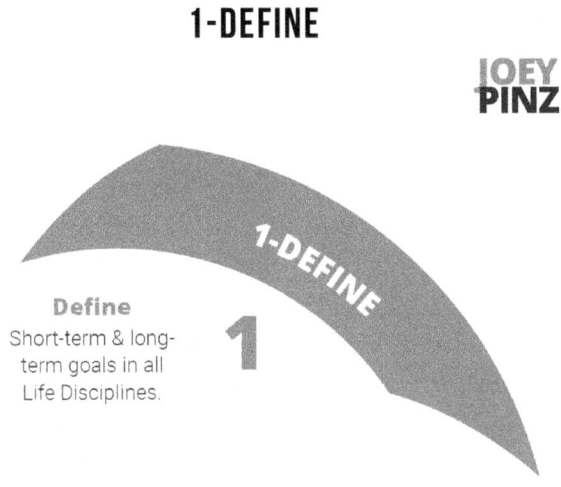

Define
Short-term & long-term goals in all Life Disciplines.

Define your goals by starting with both short-term and long-term objectives. Consider what you want to achieve in your personal life and career and write them down.

Just like defining success, it's crucial to establish short-term and long-term goals across all aspects of life. Doing so is pivotal for attaining success and happiness. Personal goals serve as guiding lights, offering direction, motivation, and a sense of purpose. They aid individuals in prioritizing time and resources toward what truly matters.

Some tips for defining personal goals:

1. Make SMART goals: Ensure goals are Specific, Measurable, Achievable, Relevant, and Time-sensitive. For instance, instead of setting vague goals like "lose weight," specify a target like "lose 20 pounds by June 1." This approach makes goals clear, achievable, and aligned with values and priorities.
2. Focus on controllable factors: It's imperative to focus on what can be controlled when setting goals. This means set-

ting goals within one's power to achieve and not overly reliant on external factors or the actions of others.
3. Reflect on values and urgency: Personal goals should be aligned with values and priorities. Reflect on what is truly important and what you value most in life.
4. Break down goals into smaller chunks or steps: Divide larger goals into manageable chunks or steps. This allows one to track progress and celebrate small wins along the way. The journey of a million miles begins with one step.
5. Be flexible, dynamic, and open to change: Life is unpredictable, and circumstances can change quickly. It's essential to remain flexible and open to change and adjust goals to stay aligned with values and priorities.

Defining personal goals is an essential step in achieving success and happiness in all four life's Disciplines. By reflecting on values and priorities, making your goals SMART, focusing on what can be controlled, breaking down goals into smaller steps, and being flexible and open to change, one can set meaningful and achievable goals that help live a fulfilling life.

2-PRIORITIZE

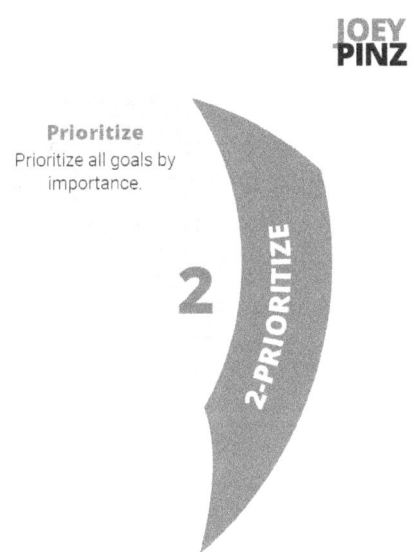

Prioritize your goals by arranging them in order of importance once you've listed them. Consider which goals will have the most significant impact on your life and focus on those first.

Prioritizing personal goals is crucial for achieving success and happiness in life's Disciplines. Here is how to go about it:

1. Determine what is most important: Take time to reflect on what one would value most in life and what one hopes to achieve in the long term. This will help determine which goals are most valuable and should be prioritized.
2. Set realistic timelines for achieving goals: Establish achievable deadlines for your goals. This means taking into account current resources and commitments and setting deadlines that are achievable but still challenging.
3. Break down goals into smaller steps: Achieving big goals can seem overwhelming, but breaking them into smaller, more manageable "bite-sized" steps can make them more achievable. This also allows one to prioritize which steps are most important and make progress toward goals systematically.

4. Celebrate small wins along the way: Achieving personal goals is a long-term process, and it's important to celebrate small wins, no matter the size, along the way. This can help keep one motivated and focused on the bigger picture.

Prioritizing personal goals is essential for achieving success and happiness in life's Disciplines. By determining what is most important, setting realistic timelines, breaking down goals into smaller steps, being willing to say "no" to distractions, and celebrating small wins, one can prioritize personal goals and progress towards achieving them.

3-DEVELOP

Develop an action plan: Create a step-by-step plan for achieving each goal. Identify the specific actions you need to take and set deadlines for each action. Here's how to do it effectively:

1. Develop a step-by-step action personal plan: Outline the specific steps that need to be taken. Identify why the specific steps are required and set deadlines for each step, and the resources needed to achieve the goal. We have a worksheet that will aid in this function, you can find it at www.joeypinz.com/book.
2. Identify resources: Determine the resources you need to achieve your goals, such as time, money, skills, and support from others. Identify what you have available and what you need to acquire.
3. Break goals into smaller objectives: Once you have defined it, break it down into smaller, manageable, and achievable objectives. This makes the overall task less daunting and allows for a more focused goal.

4. Create a detailed action plan: Develop a thorough plan that outlines the steps needed to achieve objectives, including deadlines for each step. For example, if the goal is to start a new business, the action plan might include conducting market research, developing a business plan, and securing financing.
5. Identify required resources: Identify the resources needed to achieve your goals, such as funding, equipment, or expertise. This will help to plan for any necessary investments or acquisitions necessary for success.
6. Review and revise regularly: Regularly review the action plan and revise as needed. This will help one adapt to any changes or challenges and ensure that the plan remains effective over time.
7. Set specific deadlines: Assign specific deadlines for each step of the action plan to maintain momentum. This will help to stay on track and ensure one is progressing towards the goals.

Developing a step-by-step action personal plan with deadlines and resources is essential to achieving personal and professional goals. By defining the goal, breaking it down into smaller objectives, developing a detailed action plan, identifying the resources needed, setting deadlines, and regularly reviewing and revising your plan, you can progress toward achieving the goals.

4-MONITOR

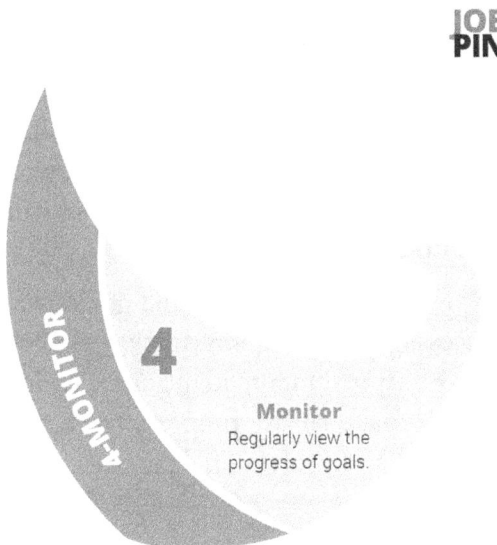

Regularly monitoring your progress toward your goals is crucial for achieving success and happiness. Without consistent assessment, it's challenging to identify improvement opportunities or maintain motivation in the face of setbacks. Here's why monitoring your goals is essential:

This is similar to improving and repeating the five simple steps to success and happiness.

1. Accountability: Regularly monitoring progress can also help one stay accountable to oneself and others. By sharing your progress with a friend, family member, or mentor, you can stay motivated and accountable for achieving your goals. Get feedback from friends and mentors. Let others look at your plan and welcome your opinions. A fresh look often results in positive results.
2. Staying on track: By regularly monitoring progress, one can stay on track and ensure that one is progressing toward goals. This can help identify where one may fall behind and take corrective action as needed.

3. Identify areas for improvement: By tracking your progress, you can identify any gaps in your knowledge or skills and take action to address these gaps.
4. Flexibility and change: Life is full of unexpected challenges and changes, and monitoring progress can help one to adapt to these changes. Regularly reviewing one's progress can adjust goals and action plans as needed to stay on track even in the face of unexpected obstacles.

Monitoring progress towards personal goals is a critical aspect of achieving success. By staying on track, celebrating successes, identifying areas for improvement, adapting to change, and staying accountable, one can make steady progress toward achieving goals and achieving personal and professional success.

5-CELEBRATE

Celebrating successes along the way, no matter how small they are, allows you to recognize and appreciate victories. Celebrating your achievements will help you stay motivated and committed to your plan.

Creating a personal plan is an ongoing process that may need to be adjusted as your circumstances change. Following these steps, you can create a personal plan to achieve your goals and develop your personal growth.

Here's why celebrating successes in important:

1. Boost motivation: Celebrating small successes can enhance and keep you focused on your goals. By monitoring progress, you can identify and celebrate even small achievements, which can help to keep you motivated and energized, and driven to continue moving forward.
2. Promote self-care and motivation: Celebrating personal success, regardless of size, is a significant aspect of self-care and

motivation. It helps to boost confidence and reminds us of our capability to accomplish our goals.
3. Simple celebrations matter: Celebrating personal success doesn't have to be extravagant. It can be as simple as treating yourself to a nice meal, taking a day off, or acknowledging your achievements. This creates a positive mindset and increases self-awareness. It can be easy to overlook our achievements, especially small ones, but taking the time to acknowledge and celebrate them is vital to our overall well-being.
4. Cultivate positivity and resilience: Celebrating personal success fosters a habit of positivity and self-reflection. It helps us view ourselves as capable and resilient individuals, building confidence in our abilities and promoting a growth mindset for future endeavors.
5. Combat societal pressures: In a society that often glorifies success and competition, it can be easy to fall into the trap of feeling like we are not doing enough or achieving enough. Celebrating personal success, no matter how small, reminds us that we are doing our best and that our efforts are worthwhile.

By taking the time to celebrate personal successes, you cultivate a culture of positivity, resilience and self-appreciation, empowering you to continue striving for your goals with confidence and determination.

5-STAGE PERSONAL PLAN WORKSHEET

Use the following worksheet to create your plan. Visit www.joeypinz.com/book to download the worksheet.

We have created a worksheet and form on www.joeypinz.com/5StagePersonalPlan

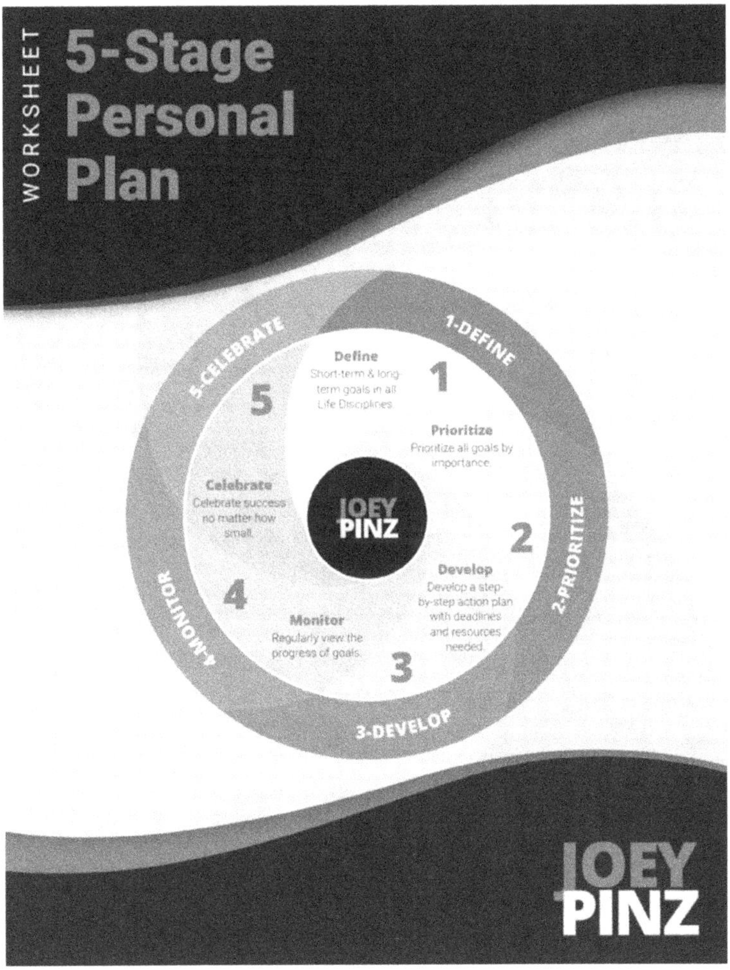

1-DEFINE: DEFINE SHORT-TERM & LONG-TERM GOALS IN ALL LIFE DISCIPLINES.

Go to www.joeypinz.com\book for the printable worksheets. Use the worksheet to define your goals in all four of the Life Disciplines.

Create your goals in the given Life Discipline as described below.

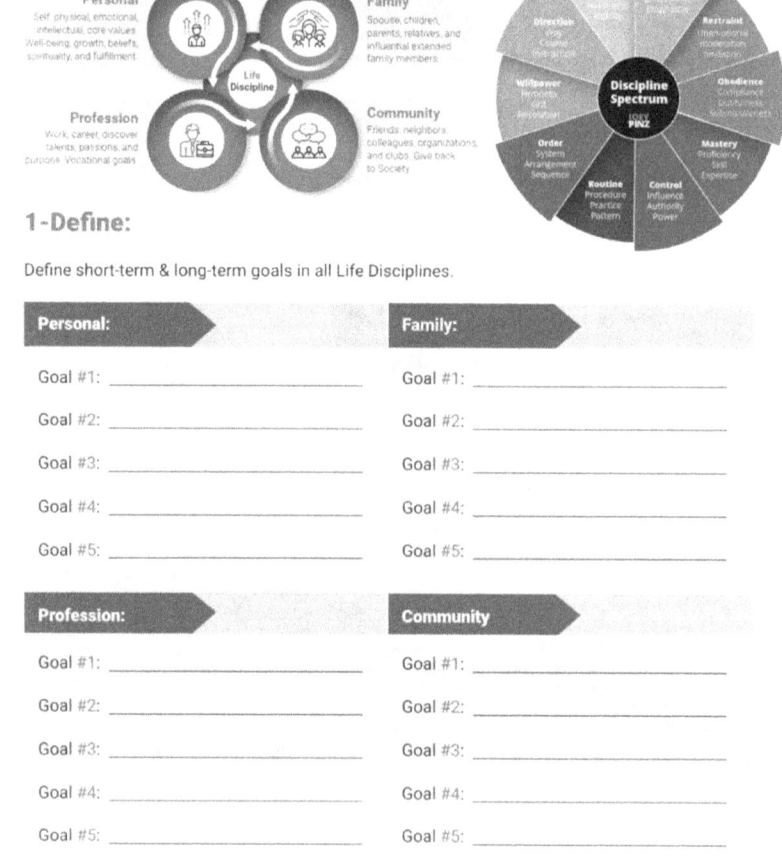

Defining short-term and long-term goals in the four life disciplines of personal, family, professional, and community can lead to a balanced and fulfilling life. Here's how to approach goal setting in each discipline:

Personal Discipline: Start by reflecting on your core values, passions, and where you see yourself in the future. Short-term goals may include adopting healthier habits, pursuing a new hobby, or improving time management. Long-term goals could focus on achieving personal growth milestones, such as enhancing emotional intelligence, completing personal projects, or attaining spiritual enlightenment. Regular self-reflection and self-care are crucial to maintaining personal discipline and achieving these goals.

Family Discipline: For family discipline, short-term goals might involve spending more quality time with family members, establishing weekly family traditions, or improving communication skills within the family. Long-term goals can aim at strengthening family bonds, such as planning for family vacations, setting up a family savings plan, or creating a family mission statement. Achieving these goals requires open dialogue, empathy, and a commitment to family well-being.

Professional Discipline: In the professional realm, short-term goals could be centered on acquiring new skills or knowledge, improving performance at work, or networking. Long-term goals may include career advancement, changing careers to better align with personal values, or achieving financial stability. Success in professional discipline often involves continuous learning, adaptability, and perseverance.

Community Discipline: Setting goals in community discipline might start with short-term objectives like attending local events, volunteering for a cause you care about, or participating in community service. Long-term goals could focus on making a significant impact in your community, leading community initiatives, or fostering a strong network of like-minded individuals. Engagement, collaboration, and a sense of responsibility are key to thriving in community discipline.

Balancing these disciplines requires identifying specific, measurable, achievable, relevant, and time-bound (SMART) goals. Regularly review and adjust these goals to ensure they remain aligned with your evolving interests, circumstances, and insights gained from life experiences. Achieving harmony across personal, family, professional, and community disciplines leads to a rich, multifaceted life filled with purpose and satisfaction.

2-PRIORITIZE

Prioritize all goals by importance. Get your goals from the first stage and add the date you will complete the goal.

Prioritizing goals across the spectrum of personal, family, professional, and community disciplines involves a strategic approach that ensures you focus on what matters most while balancing various aspects of life. After defining your goals, the next step is to arrange them by importance and assign realistic completion dates, ensuring alignment with your overall vision for life.

Start by categorizing each goal as either high, medium, or low priority. High-priority goals are those that will have the most significant positive impact on your life or are time-sensitive. Medium-priority goals are important but can be approached with more flexibility. Low-priority goals are those that you wish to achieve but can wait without significant consequences.

Use the Eisenhower Matrix to further refine your priorities by distinguishing between what is urgent and what is important. Find our Joey Pinz Eisenhower Matrix on www.joeypinz.com/EisenhowerMatrix.

This helps in focusing on goals that contribute significantly to your life's disciplines without getting overwhelmed by less impactful tasks.

Once priorities are set, assign realistic deadlines to each goal. Consider factors such as the time required to achieve the goal, available resources, and how each goal fits into your broader life plan. Setting specific completion dates not only provides a clear timeline but also serves as a motivator and helps in tracking progress.

Balancing across disciplines requires revisiting and adjusting your goals and priorities regularly. Life circumstances change, and so will your goals. Regularly review your goals to ensure they remain aligned with your personal growth and life changes. This dynamic approach ensures that you remain focused on what truly matters to you at different stages of your life.

Profession
Work, career, discover talents, passions, and purpose. Vocational goals.

Community
Friends, neighbors, colleagues, organizations, and clubs. Give back to Society.

2-Prioritize *(cont.)*

Personal	Due Date
Goal #1: _____	_____

Family	Due Date
Goal #1: _____	_____

Profession
Work, career, discover talents, passions, and purpose. Vocational goals.

Community
Friends, neighbors, colleagues, organizations, and clubs. Give back to Society.

2-Prioritize *(cont.)*

Profession	Due Date
Goal #1: _____	_____

Community	Due Date
Goal #1: _____	_____

3-DEVELOP

Develop a step-by-step action plan with deadlines. Select the elements of the Discipline spectrum needed to complete the goal. Do this for all four Life Discipline, Family, Life and Professional.

Developing a step-by-step action plan with deadlines, while incorporating elements of the Discipline Spectrum, requires a structured approach tailored to each of the four life disciplines: personal, family, professional, and community. Integrating the ten elements of the Discipline Spectrum—focus, restraint, obedience, mastery, control, routine, order, willpower, direction, and strictness—enhances the efficiency and effectiveness of achieving these goals.

Personal Discipline: Begin with setting clear personal goals that resonate with your values and vision. Incorporate Focus by dedicating specific times for goal-related activities, minimizing distractions. Use Restraint to avoid temptations that could derail your progress. Establish a Routine that supports your well-being and goal attainment, and exercise Willpower to persist through challenges.

Family Discipline: Family goals often involve complex dynamics and emotions. Apply Control to manage emotions during discussions and decision-making. Utilize Order by organizing family schedules and responsibilities for harmony. Implement Obedience in adhering to agreed-upon family rules and values, fostering a sense of security and belonging.

Professional Discipline: Professional growth is achieved through Mastery of skills and knowledge within your field. Set a Direction with career objectives that align with your long-term aspirations. Routine can be used to structure your workday for peak productivity, while Strictness ensures high standards in your work output.

Community Discipline: Engaging with the community requires Focus on issues and causes that matter most to you. Restraint is necessary to balance community involvement with other life disciplines. Willpower supports ongoing commitment to community causes, even when faced with obstacles. Lastly, Order helps in organizing community projects or events efficiently.

For each discipline, detail the steps required to achieve your goals, assigning realistic deadlines. This might include specific actions like enrolling in a course for professional mastery, setting weekly family meetings for enhanced communication, daily personal meditation for mental control, or volunteering monthly for community engagement. Regularly review and adjust your plan to reflect progress, changing priorities, and new insights. Integrating the elements of the Discipline Spectrum throughout your action plans ensures a comprehensive approach to achieving a balanced and fulfilling life.

4-MONITOR

Regularly view the progress of goals.

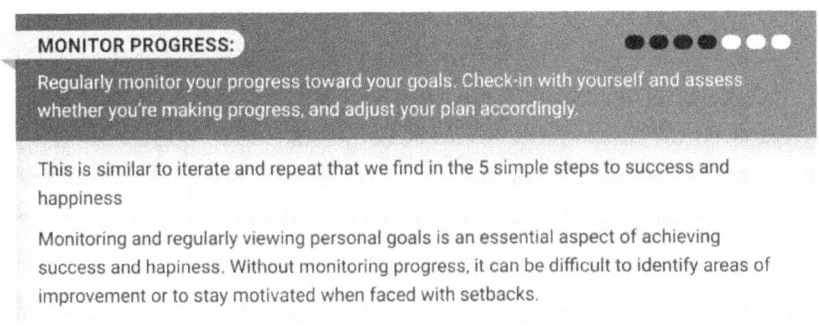

Create a process to monitor, iterate and repeat each goal. Have friends, peers, and mentors review your goals. You have created your personal success plan. You have set your goals, identified obstacles, and map out your actions. You are ready to take on the world and achieve your dreams.

Monitoring your progress is crucial in ensuring that your personal success plan works. It helps you track how far you have come, how well you are doing, and what to do next. It helps one stay focused, motivated, and accountable. It helps you celebrate your achievements and learn from your mistakes, which we learn in the last stage of a personal plan.

But how do you monitor your progress effectively? How do you measure your success and adjust your plan if needed? Here are some ways that can help you.

Another way to monitor your progress is to check in with yourself every day. You can use a journal, a planner, an app, or any other tool that works for you. Understand what you did, what went well, what didn't go well, and what you learned. Rate yourself on a scale of how satisfied you are with your progress. This will help you reflect on your actions, identify problems or gaps, and make necessary changes.

Make goal-tracking a weekly task: A third way to monitor your progress is to review your goals and actions every week. You can use this time to evaluate how far you have come, how close you are to achieving your goal, and what you need to do next.

Compare your actual performance with your expected performance and see if there are any discrepancies. This will help you assess your effectiveness, recognize your strengths and weaknesses, and adjust your plan accordingly.

Another way to monitor progress is to revise your goals as needed. Sometimes, you may find your goals too simple or ambiguous, precise, not realistic, or tiresome. You may need to change your goals to make them more exciting, evident, achievable, and exhilarating.

This will help you avoid complacency, uncertainty, and exasperation. Monitoring a personal success plan is a rewarding process that helps you stay on course, achieve your goals, and live your dreams.

We enable you to measure what matters most with precision, clearness, and reaction.

5-CELEBRATE

Record how you will celebrate each goal when achieved.

5-Celebrate

CELEBRATE SUCCESSES:
Celebrate your successes along the way, no matter how small they are. Celebrating your achievements will help you stay motivated and committed to your plan.

Remember, creating a personal plan is a dynamic process, and it may need to be adjusted as your circumstances change. By following these steps, you can create a personal plan that will help you achieve your goals and develop your personal growth.

Notes:

Set a reward system: Monitor your progress to reward yourself for completing each task or milestone. You can choose meaningful and enjoyable rewards, such as viewing a movie, purchasing something new, or spending time with friends. You can also use rewards as incentives to motivate yourself to work better.

This will help you appreciate your efforts, boost your self-confidence, and reinforce your positive habits.

Take time for self-care: One of the best ways to celebrate success is to take care of yourself. Treat yourself to something that makes you cheerful, such as a great cup of brew, a deep massage, or a new book. You can also take some time to reflect on what you have accomplished and how far you have come. This will help you appreciate your efforts, revive your energy, and boost your mood.

Spend time with loved ones: Another way to celebrate your success is to share it with the people who matter most. Invite them to join you for a special meal, a fun activity, or a heartfelt conversation. You can also express gratitude for their help, inspiration, and motivation. This will help you increase your relationships, create progressive memories, and spread enjoyment.

Show your appreciation: Celebrating success is acknowledging the people who helped you along the way. You can send them a special note, a present, or a flattering remark.

Unleash your creativity. Make something representing your achievements, such as a random collection or a poem. You can also try something new that challenges your skills, such as learning a musical instrument or a sport.

This will help you express yourself, grow individually, and discover new potential. You can also pay it forward by helping someone else who needs it.

Consider the pay-it-forward 30-day challenge. Every day for a month, pay it forward to a person or group. It's an illuminating endeavor. This will help you cultivate a giving spirit, build a network of collaborators, and inspire others to succeed.

Apply gratitude: Write down what you are thankful for, such as your assets, prospects, and lessons learned.

This will help you cultivate an optimistic mindset, attract more abundance, and increase your well-being.

Spontaneity. You can do something surprising, fun, or adventuresome, such as going on a road trip, going to a comedy show, or deep-sea fishing.

This will help you add elation, variation, and enjoyment to your life.

Celebrating completed goals in a personal success plan is a thrilling process that helps you enjoy the rewards of your challenging work. It helps you recognize how amazing you are, how much you have developed, and how much more you can do. It helps you value what matters most with gratefulness, bliss, and love. It helps you live fully, enthusiastically, and purposefully.

STEP 04 IMPROVE AND REPEAT

▶▶ **ITERATE:**
and Repeat

> Continuous improvement is better than delayed perfection.
> —Mark Twain

Improve and repeat are commonly used in problem-solving, design, and development. They refer to making changes and improvements to a product or solution based on feedback and testing.

Improve: Look to improve all facets continually of your plan. It involves refining and optimizing a design or solution based on testing or customer use feedback. Iterating aims to improve the product or solution and move it closer to its intended goal.

Repeat: To repeat means to carry out a process or action again. In the context of problem-solving or development, repeating a process often involves going back to the beginning of a cycle and starting over again. Repeating aims to identify new insights or opportunities for improvement and refine the product or solution until it meets the desired outcome.

Iteration involves incremental improvements to a product or solution based on feedback. In contrast, repeat involves returning to the beginning of a process or cycle to refine and improve the solution. Together, these processes can lead to a better product or solution that meets the intended goal.

It's important to note that all steps should be reviewed. Perhaps something has reshaped your perspective, and a new definition of success is in order.

Are you ready to take your personal success plan to the next level? It's time to embrace the power of iteration and repetition.

Iteration is all about making minor, incremental improvements over time. Instead of making significant, sweeping changes all at once, you focus on taking small steps forward. It's like climbing a staircase – you don't leap up several steps at a time, you take one step at a time, and eventually, you reach the top. It's running a marathon one stride at a time.

Regarding personal success, iteration is the key to sustainable progress. You can't expect to make massive changes overnight and see immediate results. Instead, you need to focus on making minor, consistent improvements in your life. This could mean setting aside 15 minutes daily to practice a new skill or taking one small action towards your daily goals.

The beauty of iteration is that it allows you to make and learn from mistakes. When you take small steps forward, you can reflect on what worked well and what didn't. You can adjust your approach, try new things, and eventually find a strategy that works for you.

But iteration alone isn't enough. You also need to embrace the power of repetition. Repetition means doing something over and over again until it becomes second nature. It's the key to building new habits and lasting changes in your life.

Think about learning to ride a bike. At first, it was challenging and uncomfortable. But as you practice, your brain and body form new connections. Eventually, bike riding becomes effortless – you don't have to think about it. You just do it.

The same principle applies to personal success. When you repeat positive behaviors repeatedly, they become ingrained in your psyche. You start to think and act differently without even realizing it. And that's when true transformation happens.

So how can you incorporate iteration and repetition into your personal success plan? Here are some ideas.

<u>Day</u>: Identify one small action you can take daily towards your goals. Write it down and commit to doing it consistently for the next 30 days.

<u>Week</u>: Take time to reflect on your progress each week. What worked well? What didn't? How can you adjust your approach moving forward?

Create a habit tracker to help you stay accountable. This could be a simple spreadsheet or an app, pen and paper, whatever works for you.

Surround yourself with positive influences. Seek mentors, coaches, and friends who support your goals and encourage you to continue. This can vastly improve quality of life as well.

Celebrate your successes along the way. It's essential to acknowledge your progress and credit yourself for your hard work, as discussed in the fourth stage.

Iteration and repetition are the secret ingredients to personal success. They allow you to progress steadily, learn from your mistakes, and build new habits that will serve you for years. So start small, stay consistent, and watch as your life transforms.

STEP 05 BALANCE LIFE DISCIPLINES

05

JOEY PINZ

▸▸ **BALANCE:**
Life Disciplines

> Balance is not something you find;
> it's something you create.
> —Jana Kingsford

Achieving a balance between life's personal, family, professional, and community Disciplines is challenging. It requires careful scheduling, ranking, and time management skills. Balancing these domains can bring enormous satisfaction and fulfillment to one's life, but neglecting any one of them can lead to tension, stress, and, ultimately, a lack of fulfillment.

Here are some practical tips on how to balance these Life Disciplines:

Set clear precedence. Defining what's most essential to you and where you want to focus your time and energy is vital. You may need to make tough decisions and sacrifices in certain areas, but having clear priorities will help you stay decisive and driven.

Start by writing down your top priorities in each Discipline. For example, in your personal life, your priority might be to exercise consistently, while in your professional life, your priority might be to complete a significant project. Once you've identified your priorities, create a schedule that allows you to allocate time to each domain accordingly.

Be realistic about the time you have available and prevent over-committing yourself. Schedule your chief activities first, then fill in the remaining time with other activities supporting your priorities. Remember to include downtime and self-care activities in the schedule.

Create a schedule. A schedule is a powerful tool for balancing life Disciplines. It helps you stay organized, manage time effectively, and avoid over-commitment. Start by creating a weekly or monthly schedule that includes time for personal, family, professional, and community activities. Perhaps use a calendar app to organize and prioritize these objectives.

Taking care of yourself is essential for balancing life Disciplines. Prioritizing self-care activities, such as exercise, meditation, or hobbies, can help reduce stress and improve overall well-being. Make time for self-care activities in your calendar, and treat them as non-negotiable, firm commitments. Consider self-care an investment in your health and well-being rather than a luxury.

Learn to say NO. One of the immense challenges in balancing life domains is learning to say "no." Turning down invitations or requests can be difficult, but sometimes protecting your time and energy is necessary. When saying NO to certain activities, you must prioritize and be a realist with activities. When asked to do something, take a moment to assess whether it aligns with your priorities and schedule. Suppose it doesn't, be polite but firm in your response. Explain that you're unable to commit and offer an alternative solution.

Setting boundaries is another important aspect of balancing life Disciplines. It's essential to establish clear boundaries between work and personal life, for example, to prevent work from encroaching on your personal time.

Communicate your boundaries clearly and be consistent in enforcing them. For example, if you've established a rule to avoid checking work email after a particular time, stick to it. It may take some time for others to adjust to your boundaries, but ultimately, it will help you maintain a healthy balance between different Disciplines of life.

Mindfulness is a powerful tool for balancing life Disciplines. It involves being present and fully engaged at the moment without distraction or judgment. Mindfulness can help reduce stress and improve focus, leading to better decision-making and productivity.

Incorporate mindfulness practices in daily routines, such as meditation or deep breathing exercises. When you're engaged in an activity, be fully present and avoid multitasking. By practicing mindfulness, you can improve your overall quality of life and balance between different Disciplines.

Balancing life's personal, family, professional, and community Disciplines can be challenging. Still, it's essential for a fulfilling and meaningful life., to set clear priorities, create a schedule, and learn to say NO.

BIBLIOGRAPHY

In the rich tapestry of knowledge and experience that has shaped this book, a multitude of voices have contributed, weaving their insights and stories into the fabric of its pages. The journey of learning and growth is deeply ingrained in the ethos of the Joey Pinz Discipline Conversations podcast, a platform dedicated to exploring the myriad ways in which discipline can be harnessed to better ourselves and society. This dedication to growth through learning from others has been the guiding light for the discussions that have taken place on the podcast, and subsequently, the foundation upon which this book stands.

As we transition into the bibliography section, it is important to acknowledge the vibrant spectrum of individuals who have graced the podcast with their presence. While their names have been altered to preserve privacy, the essence of their contributions remains untouched, offering invaluable perspectives that have been referenced throughout this book. These guests, coming from diverse backgrounds and professions, have shared their unique experiences and wisdom, thereby enriching the content and providing a well-rounded view on the power of discipline.

The list that follows is more than just a citation of sources; it is a homage to the collective wisdom and shared journey of exploration that these conversations have encapsulated. Each entry not only serves as a reference point for the discussions held within these pages but also stands as a testament to the profound impact that disciplined, thoughtful dialogue can have on individual and societal growth. Visit www.joeypinz.com for a deeper dive into these conversations and the remarkable individuals behind them. As you peruse this bibliography, let it be a reminder of the rich dialogue and the shared human quest for knowledge and improvement that it represents.

AALIYAH

Gender: Female
Age range: 40s
Background: American—Caucasian
Location: USA

Aaliyah is a world-renowned master attorney mediator with 25+ years of experience resolving human conflict. She has written and spoken widely to global audiences seeking a better understanding of conflict and pragmatic solutions.

MOTIVATION:

Aaliyah is motivated by the desire for self-improvement and continuous learning. She strives to be the best version of herself and constantly asks herself how much more she can expand her knowledge, curiosity, kindness, forgiveness, and understanding. She is driven to grow and gain wisdom as she ages. She shares a story about a North Vietnamese village during the Vietnam War, where doctors from the South inoculated the women and children against smallpox, which led to the men cutting off the arms of those who received the vaccine. This story reminds Aaliyah not to be too arrogant and to be mindful of the consequences of her actions.

ROLE OF DISCIPLINE:

As a master mediator, negotiator, and author who has resolved many cases involving human conflict and complex problems. She uses Discipline to listen deeply to what people are saying and not saying, how they say it, and what they feel. She also uses Discipline to temper her emotions and reactions and create synergy among diverse personalities and interests. She believes that most conflict starts with tension that can be diffused by holding a calm, which also requires Discipline.

DEFINE SUCCESS:
Defines success as resolving conflict and diffusing tension by listening profoundly and detecting lies. She believes that all conflict starts with tension and that most people are not listening but rehearsing what they want to say.

STRENGTHS:
While the guests of the podcast did not necessarily take the strength test, based on our conversation, we may infer these strengths:

- She is an expert in mediation and conflict resolution, with over 30 years of experience and a reputation for crafting creative and pragmatic solutions.
- She is keen to manage a big ego and solid personality and create synergy among diverse groups.
- She deeply understands human communication, emotions, and motivations and can detect when someone is lying or hiding something.
- She can engage her audience with exciting metaphors, examples, and stories illustrating her points.
- She is confident, assertive, charismatic, respectful, empathetic, and humble.

WHAT DOES DISCIPLINE MEAN TO YOU?
As a seasoned mediator, negotiator, and author, she has successfully resolved numerous complex conflicts and interpersonal issues. Her expertise lies in her ability to deeply listen—not just to words but to the unspoken cues, emotions, and underlying needs that individuals communicate. By maintaining emotional composure and creating harmony among diverse personalities, she uses a combination

of empathy and strategic thought to foster understanding. She also recognizes that conflict often stems from tension that can be managed by staying calm and composed—a practice that is central to her approach. Through these methods, she has fostered more effective collaboration and transformative solutions.

ANDRES

Gender: Male
Age range: 40s
Background: American – African American
Location: USA

Andres is a serial entrepreneur who started his first company in Zimbabwe when he was nine years old. Andres moved to the U.S. with only $40 in his pocket to study and started his second company. He then spent over a decade in various roles at a Fortune 500 company responsible for launching multi-million-dollar strategic new growth initiatives.

MOTIVATION:

Andres is motivated by his faith and belief in being a faithful steward of what God has entrusted him to steward. He believes that the more he is given, the more is expected of him and that growth is essential in all areas of life, including business, finance, and family. He sees commitment and consistency as the two critical factors in achieving any goal or outcome, and he applies these principles to his own life. He also recognizes that small, consistent actions over time can lead to exponential growth and success.

ROLE OF DISCIPLINE:

Discipline helps him to be social entrepreneur who identifies and solves problems with a business perspective and a social impact. He also explains the difference between a social venture and a nonprofit organization regarding their objectives, profits, and donations.

DEFINE SUCCESS:

Define success as solving a social problem with a business perspective and generating a profit that can be used for social impact. They also mention some examples of social entrepreneurs, such as Tom's Shoes. A social entrepreneur establishes an enterprise to solve social problems or affect social change.

STRENGTHS:

Strengths as a social entrepreneur are:

- He has a clear definition of what a social entrepreneur is.
- He can identify a problem he wants to solve from a business perspective but with a social impact attached.
- He can explain the difference between a nonprofit and a social venture.
- He is willing to take on the risk and effort to create positive social changes through his initiatives.

WHAT DOES DISCIPLINE MEAN TO YOU?

Discipline empowers him to excel as a social entrepreneur, allowing him to identify challenges and implement solutions that blend business acumen with social impact. He adeptly distinguishes between social ventures and nonprofit organizations, clarifying how their goals, profit models, and reliance on donations differ fundamentally. His approach combines sustainable business strategies with a commitment to positive societal change, ensuring both financial viability and meaningful impact.

ANTHONY

Gender: Male
Age range: 50s
Background: Palestinian
Location: USA

With over 20 years of legal experience, Anthony seeks to build a bridge of understanding between Islam and the West

MOTIVATION:

Anthony shares that his motivation comes from his faith in Islam, which means submission to the unseen creator of the heavens and the earth. He believes that it is arrogant of human beings who do not have an answer for where they came from and their purpose in life, not to submit to something. Anthony believes submitting to God makes him the most accessible person on earth because he does not submit to any man, status, money, habit, or influencer. He believes that everyone is a slave to something, and for him, being in connection with his creator and going back to authoritative sources like the Quran is his motivation. Anthony mentions that the Quran is an incredible book that the West should know about, and despite not believing that it comes from God, there is a consensus that it is a book promulgated 1400 years ago and maintained by Muslims as is. He contrasts this with the Bible, which is in different languages, and scholars are still deciding what was later introduced, what was a scribal mistake, and so forth. Anthony shares that Muslims live by the tenets in the Quran and that it is still being used effectively today.

ROLE OF DISCIPLINE:

Helping him to communicate his perspective and experience as a Muslim living in the United States. He believes that Discipline is needed to open up the conversation between Muslims and non-Muslims and overcome ignorance and misconceptions. He also shows respect and objectiveness in his discussion and acknowledging the world's diversity and complexity. Discipline helps him define the gap between Islam and America.

DEFINE SUCCESS:

Defines success as opening up the conversation between Muslims and Americans and reducing the ignorance and misconceptions on both sides. They also imply that success would involve a more accurate portrayal of Islam in the media and a more objective understanding of what's happening worldwide.

STRENGTHS:

His strengths include his ability to explain complex issues in an easy-to-understand manner, his extensive knowledge and understanding of Islam and the Western world, his ability to provide objective information and verifiable facts, and his willingness to engage in open and honest conversations about challenging topics. He also seems skilled at connecting historical events and ideas to current issues and problems and recognizing and addressing misconceptions and misunderstandings about Islam.

WHAT DOES DISCIPLINE MEAN TO YOU?

Discipline aids him in effectively communicating his experiences and perspectives as a Muslim living in the United States. He believes that discipline is essential in fostering open dialogue between Muslims and non-Muslims, thereby helping to overcome ignorance and dismantle misconceptions. By maintaining a respectful and objective stance, he acknowledges and embraces the world's diversity and complexity. Discipline enables him to bridge the cultural and perceptual gap between Islam and American society, fostering greater understanding and empathy on both sides.

AUBREY

Gender: Female
Age range: 40s
Background: East Europe—Caucasian
Location: USA

Aubrey is a no-nonsense business management professor (PhD.) & coach, I combine neuroscience and the transformative power of art and embodiment.

MOTIVATION:

Aubrey is motivated by the fleeting nature of time and our limited time on Earth. She wants to maximize her time and is deeply aware of the gift of every day. Her father died when she was a little girl, which made her aware that bad things can happen to good people and that one can be plucked out without doing anything wrong. This personal experience has made her appreciate life and the privilege of being spared from the wars, plagues, and famines that our ancestors faced. She believes in gratitude, chanting and appreciating what one has, and encourages people to think about what they're doing with their time. She also follows the Stoics' principle of memento mori, which is to remember that you will die and to make the most of the time you have. Hana suggests that people should think about the last time they saw their loved ones or partners, hold them tighter, kiss them warmly, and appreciate them more.

ROLE OF DISCIPLINE:

Helping her to explore the connections between science, art, and nonverbal experiences in self-discovery and self-mastery. She also draws from her diverse background in academia, business management, philosophy, and coaching to understand how we work and how we know ourselves.

DEFINE SUCCESS:

Defines success as achieving self-mastery and knowing oneself through science, art, and nonverbal experiences. They also imply that success involves balancing being self-obsessed and unaware of oneself.

STRENGTHS:

While the guests of the podcast did not necessarily take the strength test, based on our conversation, we may infer these strengths:

- She has a clear introduction and a hook that engages the listener's interest and curiosity.
- She demonstrates her expertise and credibility by mentioning her academic background, teaching experience, and coaching practice.
- She uses examples and anecdotes to illustrate her points and make them more relatable.
- She shows enthusiasm and passion for her topic and conveys a positive tone throughout her speech.

WHAT DOES DISCIPLINE MEAN TO YOU?

Discipline assists her in exploring the intricate connections between science, art, and nonverbal experiences, guiding individuals on their journey of self-discovery and self-mastery. She leverages her diverse background in academia, business management, philosophy, and coaching to provide a holistic understanding of human behavior—how we function and how we come to know ourselves. Her multidisciplinary approach enables her to weave together different perspectives, offering profound insights into personal growth and the process of self-realization.

AUDREY

Gender: Female
Age range: 40s
Background: Australia—Caucasian
Location: Australia
Author, travel writer, and blogger.

MOTIVATION:

Audrey is motivated by achieving things, helping people, and being happy, fruitful, exciting, and enjoyable. She is driven by achieving her goals, reflected in her career in leadership and helping others. She is passionate about sharing her knowledge and experiences through her website, blog, and books. Audrey believes that travel is an excellent education that changes people's perspectives on life, and she wants everyone to experience it. Audrey measures success based on the feedback she receives, whether it be positive reviews, messages, or feedback. She values both internal and external validation.

ROLE OF DISCIPLINE:

Discipline helps her learn self-control, obedience, respect for different cultures, travel more, and learn another language. She also mentions that preparing before traveling is essential, which shows her Discipline in planning and researching.

DEFINE SUCCESS:

Defines success as being able to experience and understand the culture and the people of the place they visit. They also mention that success depends on how much preparation and time they have before and during their travel. They imply that success is not just about visiting a place but also learning from it and building layers of understanding.

STRENGTHS:

While the guests of the podcast did not necessarily take the strength test, based on our conversation, we may infer these strengths:

- She has a good command of English and can express herself clearly and fluently.
- She has much travel experience and can share her insights and perspectives on different cultures and places.
- She is respectful and curious about other people's cultures and tries to learn from them.
- She is adaptable and flexible when things go wrong or unexpectedly during her travels.

WHAT DOES DISCIPLINE MEAN TO YOU?

She emphasizes the importance of developing self-control, practicing obedience, and showing respect for different cultures. She also encourages traveling more and learning another language to broaden one's perspective. Her approach reflects a commitment to discipline, particularly in the way she meticulously plans and researches before any trip, ensuring a thoughtful and respectful engagement with new environments and cultures.

AUTUMN

Gender: Female
Age range: 40s
Background: American—Caucasian
Location: USA

Autumn is a self-taught wedding floral and event designer, owner of 5 different businesses, podcast host, author, speaker, goal-getter, mother, wife, optimist, and enneagram three. She loves sharing her journey and inspiring moms to create a life they love through entrepreneurship.

MOTIVATION:

Autumn's motivation seems driven by becoming a shareholder in her business. She is Disciplined and motivated to hustle in the short term to reach this goal. Additionally, she enjoys the creative aspect of her business, particularly in floral design, which she has systemized to make it less work intensive. Autumn also stresses the importance of automation, delegation, and systemizing processes to create efficiencies and enable growth. She started her business by seeing and pursuing a need, even though she did not have the skill at the time. She then practiced, learned from others, built relationships with vendors, and created a beautiful portfolio to promote her business.

ROLE OF DISCIPLINE:

Helping her to train herself to do things in a controlled and habitual way. She has the Discipline to juggle tasks such as raising her kids, running her businesses, and building her email funnels. She also has the Discipline rules or a code of behavior that she sets for herself or follows from others. Discipline helps her goals and improves her performance.

DEFINE SUCCESS:

Defines success in business as balancing multiple responsibilities and goals, such as family, work, and personal growth. They also value Discipline, mindset, and passion as individual drivers of success. They view success as a process rather than a destination, and they have specific examples of achievements.

STRENGTHS:

While the guests of the podcast did not necessarily take the strength test, based on our conversation, we may infer these strengths:

- She is multitasking and can handle multiple responsibilities at once.
- She has a solid motivation to succeed for her kids.
- She is resourceful and can work with what she has.
- She has a growth mindset and is unsatisfied with the status quo.
- She has the Discipline and time management skills to juggle everything and prioritize the right things.

WHAT DOES DISCIPLINE MEAN TO YOU?

Discipline enables her to cultivate habits and perform tasks in a controlled, consistent manner. She demonstrates remarkable discipline in balancing various roles—raising her children, managing her businesses, and building email marketing funnels. Additionally, she follows a set of self-imposed rules or adopts structured guidance from others, ensuring she stays focused and efficient. This disciplined approach not only helps her achieve her goals but also continually elevates her performance across all aspects of her life.

AXTON

Gender: Male
Age range: 40s
Background: American – Caucasian
Location: USA

Axton is a tech industry veteran and entrepreneur. After serving in the United States Air Force, he pursued his passion for technology.

MOTIVATION:

Axton is motivated by impact, results, and finding significance. He is currently focused on using his gifts and talents as a form of worship to mankind and being a good steward of the gifts he has been given. He measures success by being aligned, grateful, and using his gifts to serve others. Axton believes that complete freedom is a recipe for disaster and that Discipline is necessary for true freedom. He has also realized that material possessions and worldly pleasures do not bring fulfillment and that true fulfillment comes from serving others. Axton's experience of living in Dubai and making money at a young age made him realize that material possessions and worldly pleasures do not bring true happiness.

ROLE OF DISCIPLINE:

Helping him to be an entrepreneur who is aggressively curious, hurdles obstacles, figures things out, focuses on solutions, and pushes for innovation. He also acknowledges that entrepreneurship requires hard work, planning, and perseverance in the face of ups and downs.

DEFINE SUCCESS:

Defines success as being aggressively curious, hurdling obstacles, figuring things out, focusing on solutions, and pushing for innovation. He also implies that success requires hard work and planning.

STRENGTHS:

Strengths that Axton has are:

- Curiosity: He describes himself as "aggressively curious" and says entrepreneurs always push for innovation and see solutions.
- Resilience: He mentions that entrepreneurs must overcome obstacles and cope with ups and downs.
- Realism: He advises people to exercise caution in their planning and not be swayed by the glorified word of an entrepreneur.

WHAT DOES DISCIPLINE MEAN TO YOU?

Discipline empowers him as an entrepreneur characterized by aggressive curiosity, a drive to overcome obstacles, and an ability to solve complex problems with a focus on innovative solutions. He understands that true entrepreneurship demands not just creativity, but also dedication, careful planning, and perseverance through the inevitable challenges. His disciplined approach allows him to navigate the ups and downs of entrepreneurship while continually pushing boundaries and pursuing meaningful innovation.

BATHSHEBA

Gender: Female
Age range: 40s
Background: Australian—Caucasian
Location: Australia

Bathsheba is a Transformational Leader and an internationally recognized Personal Branding & Online Business Specialist.

MOTIVATION

Bathsheba is motivated by human transformation and seeing people thrive. She finds success in how she feels, such as attracting the right opportunities, people, places, and synchronicities into her life. Materialistic success does not define success for her. She believes that the most successful thing she has achieved is understanding the significant role of the mind in our world as an individual and a collective.

ROLE OF DISCIPLINE:

As a personal branding expert, she uses Discipline to train herself and others to be consistent and congruent across different platforms and situations. She also uses Discipline, a system of rules and expectations that she sets for herself and her clients. Discipline helps her drive goals and build trust with her audience.

DEFINE SUCCESS:

Defines success as having a great personal brand that seems to associate success with the self-belief of giving value to others.

STRENGTH:

While the guests of the podcast did not necessarily take the strength test, based on our conversation, we may infer these strengths:

Concepts and the importance of being authentic in one's personal branding. She also emphasizes the significance of self-belief and comfort with one's natural state.

WHAT DOES DISCIPLINE MEAN TO YOU?

As a personal branding expert, she applies discipline to cultivate consistency and alignment across different platforms and contexts, both for herself and her clients. She has developed a structured system of rules and expectations that guide her actions and help maintain a cohesive brand identity. This disciplined framework is not just about achieving goals, but also about building trust and credibility with her audience, ensuring her brand consistently reflects authenticity and reliability

BETE

Gender: Female
Age range: 40s
Background: American – Caucasian
Location: USA

Bete is a human trafficking survivor, widow, former executive turned fashion designer, and influential podcaster.

MOTIVATION:

Bete is motivated by her desire to become the best version of herself and create positive societal change. She believes her podcast can unite people and help them connect despite their differences. Success means achieving balance in all areas of her life, including family, friends, finances, love, house, and health. She measures success by how well she manages to balance all these pillars in her life. Balancing all these aspects and prioritizing them is crucial, and when they all align, it makes her feel successful.

ROLE OF DISCIPLINE:

Helping Bete to express her personality and style through fashion. She believes that Discipline is needed to dress to impress and to feel empowered, beautiful, and sexy. She also shows Discipline when matching her outfits, even at the gym. She prefers to wear business attire rather than casual clothes at work. Discipline helps set her mood and how she wants to take on the day.

DEFINE SUCCESS:

Defines success as achieving their goals and feeling good about themselves. For Bete, success means feeling empowered, beautiful, and sexy by dressing to impress and viewing things differently in the office by wearing business attire. looking professional and confident in their work environment.

WHAT DOES DISCIPLINE MEAN TO YOU?

Discipline plays a key role in helping her express her personality and style through fashion. She believes that dressing with intention requires discipline—using it as a tool to not only 'dress to impress' but to feel empowered, beautiful, and confident. Her disciplined approach extends to even the smallest details, such as matching her gym outfits, showcasing her commitment to presenting her best self at all times. At work, she prefers business attire over casual clothing, using disciplined choices to set a professional tone that positively influences her mood and approach to each day.

BROOKLYN

Gender: Female
Age range: 40s
Background: East Europe
Location: East Europe

Brooklyn is a SaaS founder and business consultant with over eight years of experience. She runs a business center in China.

MOTIVATION:

Brooklyn's strongest motivation comes from the idea that she hasn't yet tried everything or achieved her potential. She enjoys doing great things and helping others. She finds it motivating to prove people wrong when they say something is impossible. Brooklyn measures success by achieving goals and setting new ones. She understands that her mindset of always striving for the next target may be a little toxic towards herself, but she enjoys the thrill of achieving new things.

ROLE OF DISCIPLINE:

It is helping her to create and sell software as a service (SaaS) platform. She believes persistence is the key to success in any new business venture and requires understanding the customer and changing the perspective.

DEFINE SUCCESS:

Defines success as being persistent and sticking with an idea until it works. She also implies that success requires understanding the customer and changing the perspective when selling software.

STRENGTHS:

While the guests of the podcast did not necessarily take the strength test, based on our conversation, we may infer these strengths:

- She speaks clearly and coherently without repeating or contradicting herself.
- She uses relevant vocabulary and grammar for the topic and context.
- She expresses her opinion confidently and convincingly, using words like "I believe" and "it requires".
- She listens actively to the interviewer, nodding and saying "yes" or "um" to show interest and understanding.

WHAT DOES DISCIPLINE MEAN TO YOU?

Discipline supports her in developing and marketing a successful Software as a Service (SaaS) platform. She emphasizes that persistence is essential for success in any new business venture, and discipline helps her maintain focus through the challenges of building and scaling a product. Additionally, she believes that understanding the customer and being adaptable—willing to change perspectives based on customer needs—are crucial for staying relevant and ensuring long-term success.

BIBLIOGRAPHY

CLAIRE

Gender: Female
Age range: 20s
Background: North Europe: Scandinavia—Caucasian
Location: Southern Europe: Italy

Claire is a professional footballer from Sweden who has played in Sweden, Switzerland, and Italy. Recently became an entrepreneur and continue to learn about being better.

MOTIVATION:

Claire is motivated to become the best version of herself. She believes that staying in her comfort zone and not taking risks is scarier than trying new things and not having them work out. Celebrating small successes and achieving small goals is also essential to her. She measures success by thinking about what her 10-year-old self would say to her and whether she would be proud of herself.

ROLE OF DISCIPLINE:

Discipline plays a role in their life by helping them to pursue their passion and goals with dedication and perseverance. They are challenging and improving their skills as a soccer player and an entrepreneur. They are also disciplined in adapting to challenges and opportunities that come with starting a business. Discipline enables them to be focused and motivated.

DEFINE SUCCESS:

Success is working hard for something, putting in many hours, and learning new things. She also mentions that being an entrepreneur is exciting because it's something new, and there's so much to learn.

STRENGTHS:

Strengths as an entrepreneur are:

- She is motivated to achieve and is willing to work hard for her goals.
- She has a nonconformity and is not afraid to try something new and different from her previous career as a soccer player.
- She has a passion for her business and enjoys learning about being an entrepreneur.
- She has teamwork skills and can collaborate effectively, as she learned from playing soccer.
- She has a street-smart ability and can deal with practical problems and challenges in her business environment.
- These are some of the typical qualities of successful entrepreneurs that Clair seems to demonstrate in her transcript. Of course, this short sample may not capture other aspects of her performance.

WHAT DOES DISCIPLINE MEAN TO YOU?

Discipline is a cornerstone in their life, driving them to pursue their passions and goals with unwavering dedication and perseverance. It supports their journey in continually honing their skills, both as a soccer player and an entrepreneur. They apply discipline to face and adapt to the unique challenges and opportunities of launching and growing a business. This disciplined mindset keeps them focused, motivated, and resilient in the face of obstacles, enabling sustained growth and achievement in both sports and entrepreneurship.

DELILAH

Gender: Female
Age range: 20s
Background: East Europe—Caucasian
Location: East Europe

Delilah is a 20+-year-old self-employed, asocial personality who could spend one year without social contact and be just fine. She trades options full time, therefore, is a digital nomad.

MOTIVATION:

Based on the conversation, Delilah's current motivation is to serve the community by helping people who may have mental issues, feel better, or maybe lonely. She believes that having people who enjoy her podcasts and videos and are educated by them motivates him now. Her motivation to serve the community came about after he realized that his full-time options trading career was not serving the community in any way.

Delilah measures success differently in different areas of her life. She measures success in her podcasts by the number of views and subscribers. In terms of working out, she measures success by how she feels after the workout, not necessarily by the number of push-ups or the time she runs. She also measures relationship success by how she feels and how the other person makes her feel.

ROLE OF DISCIPLINE:

Discipline plays a role in their life by helping them to pursue their interests and passions. They are reading books, learning new things, and creating content for their podcast. They are also disciplined in managing time and energy and choosing when and how to interact with others. Discipline allows them to be independent and self-reliant.

DEFINE SUCCESS:

Defines success as being curious and learning new things. They both have different perspectives on what makes them happy and fulfilled.

STRENGTH:

While the guests of the podcast did not necessarily take the strength test, based on our conversation, we may infer these strengths:

- She is curious and well-read, which can make her more knowledgeable and engaging.
- She has a unique perspective and personality, which can make her stand out from other podcasters.
- She can connect with her audience by being honest and authentic about herself and her opinions.

WHAT DOES DISCIPLINE MEAN TO YOU?

Discipline plays a vital role in her life, empowering her to actively pursue her interests and passions. She dedicates time to reading books, exploring new topics, and creating compelling content for her podcast. Her disciplined approach extends to effectively managing her time and energy, ensuring she can engage meaningfully with her audience while maintaining a healthy balance. Additionally, discipline grants her the independence and self-reliance necessary to make deliberate choices about when and how to interact with others, optimizing her personal and professional growth.

DIEGO

Gender: Male
Age range: 40s
Background: American – African American
Location: USA

Diego is an expert on building business value and developing a plan for success using a systematic approach for measuring and improving the value of a business. He is on a mission to shift the balance of power in favor of small and midsize business owners as they approach their transition.

MOTIVATION:

Diego is motivated by making a difference and setting an excellent example for her daughter, who is a high achiever. He wants to fulfill whatever God has put him on Earth to do and wants to pay back what he has received. Diego believes that success can be measured by the impact on others, such as helping a business grow or making the team perform better. He follows soccer and the English Premier League, and he likes to watch the top teams play because they offer more action, excitement, and skill.

ROLE OF DISCIPLINE:

Helping Diego start and grow his small business requires much freedom, innovation, and change. He also implies that Discipline is vital for improving families and communities through small businesses.

Define Success:

- The accomplishment of an aim or purpose
- The attainment of wealth, favor, or eminence
- The ability to innovate, deliver change, and improve communities

STRENGTHS:

While the guests of the podcast did not necessarily take the strength test, based on our conversation, we may infer these strengths:

- speaks fluently and confidently, without hesitations or pauses.
- uses appropriate vocabulary and grammar for the topic and context.
- expresses her opinions clearly and supports them with examples and facts.
- engages with the interviewer by asking questions and showing interest.
- uses body language and tone of voice to convey enthusiasm and emotion.

WHAT DOES DISCIPLINE MEAN TO YOU?

Supporting Diego in starting and expanding his small business demands a high level of freedom, innovation, and adaptability. He also emphasizes that discipline is crucial not only for business growth but also for uplifting families and communities through the success of small enterprises.

Diego defines success as the achievement of a specific aim or purpose, the attainment of wealth, recognition, or influence, and demonstrating the ability to innovate, drive meaningful change, and positively impact communities.

GABRIEL

Gender: Male
Age range: 30s
Background: American – African American
Location: USA

As CEO and Founder of a corporation, Gabriel has given several TEDx Talks on Discipline, Confidence, Mental Toughness & Personal Initiative and has authored 30+ books.

MOTIVATION:

Gabriel is motivated by leaving a legacy and positively impacting the world, being a role model for his children, and making his brand ubiquitous with personal and professional development. He measures success by having clear goals and consistently taking action to achieve them.

ROLE OF DISCIPLINE:

As a former professional basketball player who used his Discipline to overcome challenges and achieve his goals, he is also a CEO and founder of a company that helps entrepreneurs and athletes develop their mindset, strategy, and accountability. He has given many TEDx Talks and authored 30+ books on Discipline, mental toughness, and personal initiative. He believes that hard work is not enough to succeed; rather, one needs to have a system and a strategy that works for them.

DEFINE SUCCESS:

Defines success as achieving one's goals and desires in life and career rather than following conventional formulas or standards of success. They also imply that success requires more than hard work, such as competency, planning, and creativity. Success is also personal and may change over time.

STRENGTHS:

While the guests of the podcast did not necessarily take the strength test, based on our conversation, we may infer these strengths:

- He is a professional basketball player who went from his high school bench to a 9-year career in just five years.
- He is a pioneer in mental game mastery, helping entrepreneurs and athletes dominate their game from the inside out.
- He has given many TEDx Talks and authored 33 books on Discipline, confidence, mental toughness, and personal initiative.
- He has appeared in national campaigns with Nike, Finish Line, Wendy's, Gatorade, Buick, Wilson Sports, STASH Investments, and TIME magazine.

WHAT DOES DISCIPLINE MEAN TO YOU?

Drawing on his background as a former professional basketball player, he used discipline to navigate challenges and achieve his goals, translating these skills into his journey as a CEO and founder of a company that supports entrepreneurs and athletes in developing a strong mindset, effective strategies, and a sense of accountability. He has delivered numerous TEDx Talks and authored over 30 books focused on discipline, mental toughness, and personal initiative. He emphasizes that while hard work is crucial, true success requires having a well-structured system and a strategy tailored to one's individual needs and goals.

GERALT

Gender: Male
Age range: 50s
Background: American—African American
Location: USA

Geralt is an award-winning D&I innovator, engineering trailblazer, and philanthropist. As co-founder of an apprenticeship program – named fortune tech 500 D&I Program of the Year in 2020

MOTIVATION:

Geralt is motivated by empathy, which drives him to help others and improve the world. He believes that while there is plenty of time to rest after death, while alive, one should find something useful to do to benefit other people. Success to him means waking up every morning with a mission, having clarity, pursuing goals, and putting in the effort. He measures success based on engagement and having a purpose.

ROLE OF DISCIPLINE:

Helping him achieve his goals, follow his passion, and cope with challenges. He has worked in tech for 45 years despite facing discrimination and unfairness. He also mentions that fairness is what you make of it, which shows his Discipline in having a positive attitude and not giving up.

Discipline can also be understood as a specific branch of knowledge, learning or practice. In this sense, he has vast experience in the technology field, which he has been involved with for a long time. He probably has a lot of expertise and skills acquired through systematic training and education.

DEFINE SUCCESS:

Defines success as making their way in tech for 45 years and not feeling like a victim despite the unfairness and discrimination they faced. They also imply that fairness is what you make of it, meaning success depends on how you perceive and respond to your situation.

STRENGTHS:

While the guests of the podcast did not necessarily take the strength test, based on our conversation, we may infer these strengths:

Geralt has a strong sense of self and does not feel like a victim of discrimination. He is confident and resilient in his career. He has robust solutions to why tech has not been fair to minorities and women.

WHAT DOES DISCIPLINE MEAN TO YOU?

Discipline has played a crucial role in helping him achieve his goals, follow his passions, and overcome challenges throughout his 45-year career in the tech industry, despite facing discrimination and unfairness. He maintains that fairness is ultimately what one makes of it, illustrating his disciplined approach to staying positive and never giving up. Discipline also extends to his knowledge and expertise—he views it as a continuous pursuit of learning. His extensive experience in the technology sector has provided him with deep skills and insights acquired through years of systematic training and dedication, reflecting both his resilience and mastery in his field.

HUNTER

Gender: Male
Age range: 40s
Background: American—Caucasian
Location: Central America

One of the most sought-after teachers today, Hunter is trailblazing a new path in the world of yoga. Known for his unorthodox perspectives, his teachings aim to help as many people as possible live pain-free life so they can realize yoga's true intentions.

MOTIVATION:

Hunter mentions that he draws a great source of his inner strength from being a trailblazer. He opened up his retreat and stepped away from his old life and into this life. He feels energized by talking about his philosophy because nobody else is doing it, and it's a radical idea that gets people to stop and have conversations. For him, success is leaping, just doing it, and not caring about the results. Failure is not doing something when the purpose is knocking at the door of your heart, and you don't open the door.

ROLE OF DISCIPLINE:

He is helping them learn about the effects of stretching on their muscles and how to avoid injury. Discipline is "the practice of training people to obey rules or a code of behavior, using punishment to correct disobedience" or "a branch of knowledge, typically studied in higher education". In this context, a human might say that type of learning and behavior.

STRENGTHS:

While the guests of the podcast did not necessarily take the strength test, based on our conversation, we may infer these strengths:

- He has a deep understanding of the anatomy and physiology of the human body and how yoga affects it
- He has a unique perspective on why stretching can be harmful and how to practice yoga safely and effectively.
- He has a sense of humor and can make his listeners laugh with his jokes and anecdotes.
- He is passionate about yoga and sharing his knowledge and experience with others.

WHAT DOES DISCIPLINE MEAN TO YOU?

He is guiding them in understanding the impact of stretching on their muscles and how to prevent injuries effectively. In this context, discipline can be seen as the practice of systematically training individuals to follow certain rules or standards of behavior, or as a specific area of expertise often explored in depth through higher education. Through this disciplined approach, he emphasizes structured learning and behavioral improvement, helping them build both knowledge and practical skills to support their well-being.

JOSEPHINE

Gender: Female
Age range: 40s
Background: American – Caucasian
Location: USA

When it comes to navigating the ins and outs of the business, Josephine has seen it all: From successful startups with brand-new ideas to well-established Fortune 500 companies.

MOTIVATION:

Josephine is motivated by making an impact and seeing that she's making a difference. She loses motivation when she is in situations where she does not see any change or people are giving lip service to leadership. She measures success by how she feels. She knows she is going in the right direction if she feels fulfilled. She knows she must do something if she feels anxious or stuck. Josephine writes quickly and does not have a fear of blank pages. She believes starting is essential; even if the first page is deleted, it breaks through the blank page. She suggests letting go of perfectionism and just starting because it does not matter if the starting material gets included.

ROLE OF DISCIPLINE:

She believes in having a clear vision of where she wants to go and how to get there. She also values involving others in her journey and listening to their ideas. Discipline helps her stay focused on her goals and avoid distractions or detours.

DEFINE SUCCESS:

Defines success as having a clear vision of where they want to go, a mission of how they will get there, and a purpose of why they exist.

They also imply that success involves getting people involved and aligned with their vision.

STRENGTHS:

While the guests of the podcast did not necessarily take the strength test, based on our conversation, we may infer these strengths:

Strengths can be inferred from her response to the question about the importance of vision in a business. She demonstrates a strong understanding of the critical role of a clear vision in achieving results and getting people to follow you. She also shows the ability to communicate complex ideas in a simple and relatable way, using a metaphor of a car trip to explain the importance of having a vision. Additionally, she mentions the three categories that organizations use, showing a deep understanding of organizational strategy and structure. Therefore, her strengths can be summarized as strategic thinking, communication skills, and expertise in organizational development.

WHAT DOES DISCIPLINE MEAN TO YOU?

She believes in having a clear vision of her destination and the steps needed to reach it, valuing the involvement of others along the way and being open to their ideas. Discipline plays a crucial role in keeping her focused on her goals, helping her stay on course and avoid unnecessary distractions or detours

BIBLIOGRAPHY

KINSLEY

Gender: Non-Binary
Age range: 40s
Background: American – Caucasian
Location: USA

Kinsley is a non-binary world-record-holding strength athlete, ranked in the sport of strongman, a business owner in the sales tech space, and a published author. Kinsley grew up overseas on military bases and lived fairly nomically throughout the U.S. before settling in the Mountain West.

MOTIVATION:

Based on the conversation, what inspires Kinsley is seeing how much they can do and how much they can help other people do too. They want to push themselves to the farthest points of their abilities and have a good life that changes from moment to moment for her. They measure success differently daily, but overall, they consider a good life to be one where she has good connections, much love from the people around them, and enough financial stability to feel safe.

ROLE OF DISCIPLINE:

Discipline plays a significant role in their life. It helps them cope with the unpleasant and challenging situations they encounter personally and professionally. It also helps them to improve their skills and performance by learning from their mistakes and taking corrective actions. Discipline Helps them to grow as a person and as a professional.

DEFINE SUCCESS:

Defines success as growing from discomfort, embracing difficulties, accessing humanity, and building trust.

STRENGTH:

While the guests of the podcast did not necessarily take the strength test, based on our conversation, we may infer these strengths:

As a speaker who gave a TEDx talk about embracing the difficulties and challenges in life and work, they are also a non-binary, sober, world-record-holding strongman competitor and published author specializing in cultivating mental toughness.

Some of their strengths are:

- They are confident and assertive about their identity and pronouns.
- They are knowledgeable and passionate about their topic of interest.
- They can connect with the audience by using examples and anecdotes from their own experience.
- They are resilient and persistent in overcoming obstacles and achieving their goals.

WHAT DOES DISCIPLINE MEAN TO YOU?

Discipline plays a significant role in their life, enabling them to manage both personal and professional challenges effectively. It helps them navigate difficult situations, improve their skills, and enhance their performance by learning from mistakes and taking corrective actions. Ultimately, discipline fosters their growth as both an individual and a professional.

LEILANI

Gender: Female
Age range: 40s
Background: America
Location: USA

Leilani is a woman who has lived two lives in one lifetime. The first part was a life of childhood abuse and trauma which grew into the full-blown disease of alcoholism. Her life was out of control, and I was circling the drain. The second part is about life today and how she urgently worked through her past and now has a beautiful life.

MOTIVATION:

Leilani used to be motivated by money because it gave her a sense of control and power and allowed her to escape the negative aspects of her life. However, she eventually realized that money was not fulfilling, and now she seeks motivation from the people she surrounds herself with, particularly those who think as she does. Leilani also expressed her desire to write another book and share more about her journey, especially the parts that were once seen as bad but have now become her strength. She mentioned that some of these topics might not be considered normal, but they are vital to her and others seeking sexual liberation without judgment. Leilani also believes in connecting with like-minded individuals who share similar values and beliefs and that expressing oneself fully without fear of judgment is important.

ROLE OF DISCIPLINE:

Helping her to overcome the challenges and traumas of her past and to share her story with courage and clarity. She also uses therapy and writing to heal and empower herself and others who may feel alone or hopeless.

DEFINE SUCCESS:

Define success as overcoming childhood abuse, trauma, and alcoholism and finding a sense of self and survival.

STRENGTHS:

While the guests of the podcast did not necessarily take the strength test, based on our conversation, we may infer these strengths:

- She has a prevailing sense of self and survival.
- She has been able to tell her story with clarity and honesty.
- She has sought therapy to heal from her past wounds.
- She has not let the negative opinions of others define her.

WHAT DOES DISCIPLINE MEAN TO YOU?

Discipline helps her overcome the challenges and traumas of her past, enabling her to share her story with courage and clarity. She also utilizes therapy and writing as tools for healing, empowering herself and inspiring others who may feel alone or hopeless.

LELAND

Gender: Male
Age range: 50s
Background: American—Caucasian
Location: USA
Leland, a long-time podcaster and publicist.

MOTIVATION:

According to Leland, money is not what motivates him. He believes that defining success is crucial to understanding what motivates a person. He is very structured and believes that motivation comes from within. As for measuring success, he suggests that it depends on how one defines it.

ROLE OF DISCIPLINE:

As a publicist, podcaster, speaker, author, blogger, and broadcaster who works in the sports and entertainment industry, he uses Discipline to overcome adversity in all shapes and sizes, such as having two open-heart surgeries, two strokes, a motorcycle accident and being hospitalized by Covid. He also uses Discipline helpful and humorous presentations that give takeaways to his audience and make them feel something. He believes that discipline can help the best version of themselves and achieve their goals.

DEFINE SUCCESS:

Defines success as controlling as much as you want in the music industry and not complaining about the system's flaws. He also implies that success is related to monetizing your music through streaming platforms. Success in the music industry can be defined differently depending on your goals, skills, and values. Some possible ways to define success are:

- Having a loyal fan base that supports your music and engages with you
- Making a living from your music through various income streams
- Creating music that expresses your artistic vision and satisfies your creative needs
- Collaborating with other musicians or producers that inspire you and challenge you
- Reaching a wider audience through exposure on media platforms or live performances
- Having a positive impact on society or culture through your music
- Receiving recognition or awards from peers or industry professionals

STRENGTHS:

While the guests of the podcast did not necessarily take the strength test, based on our conversation, we may infer these strengths:

- He is a podcast veteran with much knowledge and insight about the music industry.
- He is optimistic and realistic about the opportunities and challenges for independent artists.
- He is confident and articulates in expressing his opinions and arguments.
- He is passionate and enthusiastic about music and creativity.

WHAT DOES DISCIPLINE MEAN TO YOU?

As a publicist, podcaster, speaker, author, blogger, and broadcaster in the sports and entertainment industry, he relies on discipline to overcome a wide range of adversities, including two open-heart surgeries, two strokes, a motorcycle accident, and a severe battle with Covid. Discipline also guides him in creating engaging and humorous presentations that provide valuable takeaways and resonate emotionally with his audience. He firmly believes that discipline can help others become the best version of themselves and achieve their goals.

MICAH

Gender: Male
Age range: 30s
Background: American – South Asian
Location: USA

Micah was born in Malaysia and lived in several countries before moving to the States. While in the States, his goal has been to build and operate his own business, an award-winning advertising agency.

MOTIVATION:

When traveling, Micah is motivated by building things, continuous problem-solving, and experiencing different cultures and foods. He measures success through retention rates, account signs, and how clients feel about the agency. He believes that marketing is just as important as sales, and outsourcing marketing may benefit some companies but not others. It depends on the brand; media spend, and size.

ROLE OF DISCIPLINE:

He believes in the power of digital marketing and content creation for any business. He also values using free tools and building a following online. Discipline helps him stay updated on the latest trends and strategies in his field and deliver quality results for his clients.

<u>Define Success:</u>

Success in digital marketing can mean different things to different organizations, but some common ways of measuring it are:

- User engagement: how users interact with your online content and channels
- Conversion funnel: how users move from awareness to action (such as purchase, sign-up, etc.)

- Brand perception: how users view your organization's identity and reputation
- Internal collaboration: how well your team works together to achieve digital marketing goals
- Customer service processes: how you handle user feedback and complaints
- SMART goals: specific, measurable, achievable, relevant and time-bound objectives for your digital marketing efforts

Digital marketing as being online, creating content, building a following, and running paid ads. They also mention organic reach and engagement as important factors.

STRENGTHS:

While the guests of the podcast did not necessarily take the strength test, based on our conversation, we may infer these strengths:

Their strengths include his knowledge and expertise in digital marketing, particularly in search engine optimization (SEO) and paid advertising. He emphasizes the importance of having an online presence and building a following through organic reach and engagement. Hemant can provide examples of businesses successfully utilizing digital marketing strategies, including doctors in rural areas targeting potential patients through Geo-targeted paid ads. He is also knowledgeable about the pros and cons of SEO and advertising and can provide insight that can linger effectively together. Additionally, Hemant stays current with industry changes and trends, such as the iOS change affecting e-commerce businesses.

WHAT DOES DISCIPLINE MEAN TO YOU?

He believes strongly in the power of digital marketing and content creation as essential tools for any business, and values leveraging free tools to build an online following. Discipline keeps him up-to-date with the latest trends and strategies, enabling him to consistently deliver quality results for his clients.

ODIN

Gender: Male
Age range: 40s
Background: American—Caucasian
Location: USA

Odin is the CEO of a leading provider of an online education platform—also a nonfiction author.

MOTIVATION:

Odin mentions that he is motivated by having an impact, mainly wanting to impact millions of people. However, he wonders how much of that motivation is ego-driven versus genuine desire. He also wants to live a life with no regrets and be financially stable to leave a legacy for future generations. Odin believes that success is measured differently in each area of life, such as revenue in business or effort in personal accomplishments. Ultimately, success is feeling proud of the effort put in.

ROLE OF DISCIPLINE:

As a CEO, entrepreneur, and speaker who has overcome challenges and achieved success personally and professionally. He uses Discipline to pursue his goals and passions, such as running, tennis, skiing, and legal education. He also uses Discipline skills and improves himself, such as hiring a coach to help him tell stories for his TEDx talk. He believes discipline can help work through their fears and live a fulfilling life.

DEFINE SUCCESS:

Defines success as accomplishing an aim or purpose, such as giving a keynote speech at a legal tech conference or doing a TEDx talk. They also mention some indicators of success, such as fame, wealth, social status, or being good at solo sports.

STRENGTHS:

While the guests of the podcast did not necessarily take the strength test, based on our conversation, we may infer these strengths:

- Running: He says he was always good at running and sounds confident about it.
- Tennis: He mentions tennis as one of the solo sports he was good at, and he seems to enjoy it.
- Skiing: He also mentions skiing as a solo sport he excelled at and sounds happy about it.
- Storytelling: He says that working with a coach to learn how to tell stories was as fun or even more fun than doing the TEDx talk. He also speaks with enthusiasm and detail about his experience.

WHAT DOES DISCIPLINE MEAN TO YOU?

For Odin, discipline is both a persistent challenge and a driving force in his life. He views discipline not just as a means to achieve goals but as a critical factor in maintaining consistency, particularly with exercise and personal well-being. Odin acknowledges that while he has demonstrated discipline in professional areas—such as leading his company, writing a book, and serving as EO president—his struggle lies in applying that same rigor to daily habits like physical activity. He reflects on how discipline can sometimes feel exhausting, yet recognizes that when he's disciplined, especially with exercise, he feels happier and more accomplished. Ultimately, David sees discipline as essential for living a life without regrets, enabling him to stay focused and intentional in both personal and professional pursuits.

OLIVER

Gender: Male
Age range: 40s
Background: American—Caucasian
Location: USA

Oliver is a Wealth Advisor and owner of a wealth management company. He specializes in helping clients with retirement planning. He helps clients create retirement plans and manage their investments.

MOTIVATION:

Oliver is motivated by his family, especially his children. As he has built his business, he has been motivated to help many people, but now he is focused on spending more time with his family and caring for his health. Oliver measures success by setting goals at the beginning of the year and looking back to see if he has achieved them. He also looks at industry numbers and compares himself to other successful advisors to ensure he delivers value to his clients and impacts their lives.

ROLE OF DISCIPLINE:

He is a wealth advisor who helps people with investing and financial planning. He needs Discipline as a branch of knowledge because he has to be familiar with different aspects of finance and economics. He also needs to have a Disciplineing practice because he has to follow specific rules and regulations in his profession, such as being a fiduciary and disclosing any conflicts of interest. He may also need to discipline himself oDisciplinents to manage their money and spending habits.

DEFINE SUCCESS:

Defines success as the attainment of wealth, favor, or eminence, as well as the accomplishment of one's goals. They also imply that success involves helping people with investing and financial planning, and being a fiduciary means putting their client's interests ahead of their own.

STRENGTHS:

While the guests of the podcast did not necessarily take the strength test, based on our conversation, we may infer these strengths:

- He has a good reputation and invokes confidence and trust by being a fee-only financial planner and a fiduciary.
- He takes a proactive approach by explaining his title and what he does for his clients.
- He is an experienced financial professional who knows the difference between wealth management and financial advising.
- He takes a holistic view of his client's finances by helping them with investing and financial planning.

WHAT DOES DISCIPLINE MEAN TO YOU?

He is a wealth advisor specializing in investing and financial planning, requiring discipline both as a branch of knowledge and as a practical skill. He must be well-versed in various aspects of finance and economics, while also adhering to the rules and regulations of his profession, such as acting as a fiduciary and disclosing conflicts of interest. Additionally, he disciplines himself in managing his own money and spending habits to set an example for his clients.

ROCKSON

Gender: Male
Age range: 30s
Background: Europe Western – Caucasian
Location: USA

Rockson is a cloud-certified full-stack developer who speaks to professionals who struggle to find meaning in life.

MOTIVATION

Rockson's primary motivation is to help others unlock their potential and achieve their goals. He finds fulfillment in coaching and guiding people who feel disconnected or struggle to balance their personal and professional lives. Rockson values authenticity and staying true to his core values, which he believes is the key to success. He measures success by the degree to which he is authentic and stays true to his values. Additionally, he believes that doing hard things and playing the long game is necessary for avoiding future pain and achieving long-term success.

ROLE OF DISCIPLINE:

Helping Rockson to cope with his mental health issues and trauma. He believes that Discipline is needed to be curious about oneself, to ask questions, and to work with the answers. He also shows Discipline support from a therapist when needed and sharing his insights and experiences with others. Discipline helps him grow as a person.

DEFINE SUCCESS:

Defines success as being able to get curious about themselves, ask questions, work with the answers, and make changes based on those answers. They also mention having support around them and releasing pain as part of their definition of success.

STRENGTHS:

While the guests of the podcast did not necessarily take the strength test, based on our conversation, we may infer these strengths:

His strengths include articulating his thoughts and ideas clearly and effectively. He can also use personal experiences to provide insight into mental health issues and the importance of vulnerability. Additionally, he can empathize with others and understand the different struggles that different people face and the societal expectations that contribute to those struggles.

WHAT DOES DISCIPLINE MEAN TO YOU?

Discipline helps Rockson cope with his mental health challenges and trauma. He believes that discipline is essential for self-reflection—encouraging curiosity about oneself, asking meaningful questions, and working with the answers. He also demonstrates discipline by seeking support from a therapist when needed and by sharing his insights and experiences with others. This disciplined approach is key to his personal growth.

RUBY

Gender: Female
Age range: 40s
Background: American—Caucasian
Location: USA

Ruby is a multi-published author and speaker who writes and speaks about diverse topics ranging from faith and spirituality to motherhood, parenting, and family to grief and loss. She writes and speaks about her life experience of disability and being legally blind yet striving to thrive and overcome.

MOTIVATION:

Ruby is motivated to write because she is passionate about it and feels called to do it. She also applies this attitude to life, not giving up and not quitting. She believes in doing her best and figuring things out when she can't move the mountain. She thinks that if something matters to a person, they will find ways to be creative, think outside the box, and be resourceful. Ruby measures success by contributing, providing love and good in the world, trying to improve it, and influencing and changing it. She thinks that success depends on a person's definition and interpretation.

ROLE OF DISCIPLINE:

As an author, speaker, and mother who inspires and empowers people to overcome their tribulations, find hope, and heal in various areas of life, she uses Discipline to cope with her lifelong disability of legal blindness, divorce, and the death/loss of her beloved husband at 38. She also uses Discipline about her heartfelt meditations on her passions related to her life experiences, such as her disability, faith, motherhood, grief and loss, solo parenting, and empowerment. She believes that discipline can help Discipline about much tribulation to thriving in all things.

DEFINE SUCCESS:

Defines success as making it work with what they have and being grateful for the opportunity to do what they love. They also attribute their success to their faith and God's healing. They don't focus on the challenges or difficulties of being legally blind but rather on the practice and experience they have gained over their lifetime.

STRENGTHS:

While the guests of the podcast did not necessarily take the strength test, based on our conversation, we may infer these strengths:

- She is a successful author despite her visual impairment.
- She has a positive and resilient attitude toward her challenges.
- She has a strong faith and belief in God's healing power.
- She has a lot of experience and practices coping with her condition.

WHAT DOES DISCIPLINE MEAN TO YOU?

As an author, speaker, and mother, she inspires and empowers others to overcome their challenges and find hope and healing across various aspects of life. Discipline has been a crucial tool for her in coping with her lifelong disability of legal blindness, as well as the hardships of divorce and the loss of her beloved husband at the age of 38. She also applies discipline to her heartfelt reflections on her experiences, including her disability, faith, motherhood, grief, solo parenting, and her journey toward empowerment. She believes that discipline is key to transforming tribulations into thriving in all areas of life.

SAVANNAH

Gender: Female
Age range: 60s
Background: American – African American
Location: USA

Savannah was the only African American student in elementary school, with only 8 African Americans in her graduating high school class. Despite her creativity and talent, she faced bullying, racial prejudice, and isolation at school due to her skin color.

Later embarking on a 32-year career teaching Fashion Marketing at a state university. She developed numerous anti-bullying programs and was recognized for excellence in teaching at the state and national levels.

At age 57, (10 years ago), I became a competitive amateur sprinter.

MOTIVATION:

Savannah is motivated because she is lucky to be alive and has been given many opportunities. She wants to help others live their best lives and find the meaning of their lives. Savannah believes that all talents and skills are meant to be shared with others to help them along the way. She measures success differently, from doing small things like helping an old lady in a parking lot to bigger things like making it to the national finals or seeing her students succeed in their careers. Savannah encourages people to stop comparing themselves to others and appreciate their accomplishments, big or small.

ROLE OF DISCIPLINE:

Helping her to cope with bullying and racial discrimination. She has the Discipline to train herself to do things in a controlled and habitual way1, such as working as an executive in a downtown store. She also has the Discipline or a code of behavior that she sets for herself or follows from others, such as handling demanding customers professionally and respectfully. Discipline helps her Discipline thick skin and overcome challenges.

DEFINE SUCCESS:

Defines success as accomplishing an aim or purpose, such as overcoming bullying, growing a thick skin, working as an executive, and handling demanding customers. They also imply that success involves hard work, resilience, and self-confidence.

STRENGTHS:

While the guests of the podcast did not necessarily take the strength test, based on our conversation, we may infer these strengths:

- She is charismatic, highly energetic, and entertaining.
- She is a nationally recognized, award-winning educator who provides teachers, parents, and administrators with the tools and confidence they need to create a culture of civility throughout school communities.
- She is a former fashion and retail executive who taught fashion marketing and career exploration/personal finance classes.
- She is an actor who has performed in shows.
- She is a sprinter who competes in senior games and holds state records for the 50 and 100 meters.

WHAT DOES DISCIPLINE MEAN TO YOU?

Discipline helps her cope with bullying and racial discrimination, enabling her to manage challenges with resilience and determination. She uses discipline to train herself to maintain a controlled, habitual approach to her responsibilities, such as working as an executive in a downtown store. Additionally, she follows a personal code of behavior, handling demanding customers with professionalism and respect. This disciplined approach has helped her develop a thick skin and overcome the obstacles she faces.

SOPHIE

Gender: Female
Age range: 20s
Background: Europe UK – Caucasian
Location: Australia

Sophie is here to inspire women to lead a life full of pleasure in every area of their life by embracing their cycles, emotions, business, and dreams. This world needs more female leaders, founders, and millionaires; embracing the woman you are is the only way.

MOTIVATION:

Sophie is motivated by seeing people follow what they want to do in their lives, and she loves it when people go against the norm and do what they want to do. She likes to see her friends succeed and build each other up. Sophie measures her success by how she feels and whether her actions and those around her support her. The driven businesswoman in her would naturally think of finances, but she has learned that it is not always the case.

ROLE OF DISCIPLINE:

She believes in being confident and empowered as a woman who speaks openly about her sexuality. She also values not letting other people's opinions or judgments affect her self-worth. Discipline helps her stay true to herself and her vision and not compromise on her integrity or authenticity.

DEFINE SUCCESS:

Defines success as being able to speak about her sexual partnerships and relationships openly and embodying her sexuality in her business. She also seems to value respect and empowerment for sexually promiscuous women.

STRENGTHS:

While the guests of the podcast did not necessarily take the strength test, based on our conversation, we may infer the following:

Their strengths include her advocacy for women and her belief in the power of embodying sexuality in business. She also has sales experience and believes she has a superpower in reading people and asking challenging questions due to her perceived softer approach as a woman. Additionally, she has a strong sense of self-worth and does not let slut shaming affect her.

WHAT DOES DISCIPLINE MEAN TO YOU?

She believes in the importance of being confident and empowered as a woman who openly speaks about her sexuality. She values maintaining her self-worth without being influenced by others' opinions or judgments. Discipline plays a crucial role in helping her stay true to herself and her vision, ensuring she never compromises her integrity or authenticity.

VALENTINA

Gender: Female
Age range: 40s
Background: Northern Europe—UK—Caucasian
Location: Northern Europe—Scandinavia

Valentina is passionate about helping perimenopausal and menopausal women regain their sparkle in life and reclaim their health through evidence-based nutrition and lifestyle modifications using the functional medicine approach.

MOTIVATION:

Valentina is motivated by helping people, particularly women, and seeing how her message can turn their lives around. She finds it rewarding to hear from people how she has helped them and measures her success by the number of women she can help. She believes helping people can positively impact society, and she enjoys receiving feedback from people who have benefited from her work.

ROLE OF DISCIPLINE:

She is a nutritional therapist who helps people with health and wellness using nutritional science and lifestyle modifications. She needs Discipline as a branch of knowledge because she must study and apply nutritional science to different cases and scenarios. She also needs to have Discipline training and practice. She must follow specific guidelines and standards in her profession, such as providing evidence-based advice and respecting client confidentiality. She may also need to discipline herself regarding stress management and mindset.

DEFINE SUCCESS:

Defines success as achieving health and wellness using nutritional science and therapy. They also mention how nutrition affects their mind and how they experience life.

STRENGTHS:

Strengths as a nutritional therapist are:

- She clearly and concisely defines what a nutritional therapist does, which helps explain her role and expertise to potential clients or collaborators.
- She emphasizes the holistic and individualized approach of nutritional therapy, which shows that she is attentive to the needs and preferences of each person she works with.
- She demonstrates her knowledge and passion for nutrition and its effects on health and wellness, which can inspire trust and confidence in her services.
- She shares her personal story and background to connect with her audience and show how she became interested in nutrition and hormones, which can make her more relatable and authentic.

WHAT DOES DISCIPLINE MEAN TO YOU?

She is a nutritional therapist who supports people in achieving health and wellness through nutritional science and lifestyle modifications. Discipline is essential for her as a branch of knowledge, requiring her to study and apply nutritional science to a variety of cases. She also relies on discipline in her training to adhere to professional standards, such as providing evidence-based advice and maintaining client confidentiality. Additionally, she disciplines herself in areas such as eating habits, stress management, and maintaining a positive mindset to serve as a role model for her clients.

WESTON

Gender: Male
Age range: 50s
Background: American—Caucasian
Location: USA

Weston is an attorney and entrepreneur who led his own firm with tremendous growth, making it one of the very rare law firms ever to make the Inc 5000 list.

MOTIVATION:

Matthew Weston, a lawyer, is motivated by his love for work and his desire to build and grow things. He comes from a family of farmers, and the saying in his law firm is "the farmer's footsteps," which means that management by walking around helps to manage and improve the business. Weston loves people and loves to see them succeed. His core values include believing and protecting dreams and creating solutions for clients. He measures success through key performance indicators, such as 30 percent growth per year, and also by the success of his team and family. He enjoys working and does not take many days off because he loves what he does.

ROLE OF DISCIPLINE:

Discipline plays a role in their life by helping them plan and anticipate the potential risks and challenges their business might face. They are Disciplined in lending legal advice and guidance tailored to their client's needs and goals. They are also disciplined in creating resources and tools to help other business owners protect their assets and interests. Discipline enables them to be real and trustworthy.

DEFINE SUCCESS:

Defines success as achieving their goals, helping their clients, and providing value to their business. They also mention some factors that can contribute to success, such as experience, heart, and planning.

STRENGTHS:

Strengths as an attorney are:

- He is passionate about his job and wants to help small to medium business owners with their legal needs.
- He has compassion for his clients and does not try to sell them unnecessary services.
- He has excellent communication skills and can explain complex legal concepts in simple terms.
- He has good research skills and can provide valuable client resources, such as the strongly protected business checklist.
- He has the creativity and can tailor his legal advice to different situations and stages of business growth.
- These are some of the typical traits of successful attorneys that Weston seems to demonstrate in his transcript. Of course, this short sample may not capture other aspects of his performance.

WHAT DOES DISCIPLINE MEAN TO YOU?

Discipline plays a vital role in their life, helping them plan ahead and anticipate the potential risks and challenges their business may encounter. They apply discipline when providing legal advice and guidance, ensuring it is tailored to each client's needs and goals. Additionally, they are disciplined in developing resources and tools that help other business owners protect their assets and interests. This disciplined approach allows them to be genuine and trustworthy in their professional endeavors.

CONCLUSION

As we arrive at the conclusion of our journey through the realms of discipline, its spectrum, and the steps to harness it for success and happiness, it's essential to reflect on the essence of what we've explored. This book, inspired by the countless insightful conversations on the Joey Pinz Discipline Conversations podcast, has been a voyage into the heart of discipline as the cornerstone of personal growth and societal betterment. Through the detailed exploration across different facets of life—personal, family, professional, and community—we've seen the multifaceted nature of discipline and its profound impact on our lives.

In Chapter 1, we embarked on an exploration of Life Disciplines, dissecting how discipline acts as the silent undercurrent guiding our personal evolution, family bonds, professional achievements, and community engagement. It's here that we laid the groundwork, understanding that discipline is not just a trait but a practice, intertwined deeply with our daily lives.

Chapter 2 unfolded the spectrum of discipline, revealing it to be far more than a monolithic concept. From focus to strictness, we delved into the various aspects of discipline, understanding how each plays a pivotal role in shaping our approach to challenges and aspirations. This spectrum serves as a testament to the complexity and richness of discipline, highlighting its role as both a guide and a guardian in our pursuit of mastery and control over our actions and destinies.

In Chapter 3, we transitioned into a practical guide with the "5 Steps to Success and Happiness." This section was not just about theoretical insights but offered a concrete plan to apply the lessons of discipline to achieve a balanced and fulfilling life. From defining success to balancing life disciplines, the steps outlined are a blueprint for anyone looking to harness the power of discipline in their journey towards personal and professional fulfillment.

This book, and by extension the conversations that have fueled its content, is a call to action—a prompt to recognize and embrace discipline in all its forms. It's an invitation to explore the depths of our own potential, to challenge ourselves, to set forth on a path of disciplined pursuit towards our goals. The disciplines discussed are not just principles but tools, each serving a unique purpose in the crafting of a life well-lived.

As we close this chapter, remember that the journey of discipline is ongoing. The stories, insights, and strategies shared here are but waypoints on a much larger path. It's a path that we walk together, learning from each other, inspired by the guests who've shared their wisdom on the Joey Pinz Discipline Conversations podcast, and driven by a shared vision of growth through learning from others.

In embracing discipline, we open ourselves to a world of possibilities. The discipline is both the journey and the destination—a spectrum of practices that guide us, challenge us, and ultimately lead us to a place of balance, success, and happiness. As you move forward, carry with you the lessons learned, the disciplines explored, and the commitment to continual growth. The journey doesn't end here; it evolves, inviting us to engage, reflect, and act with discipline at the heart of all we do.

May this book serve not as an ending but as a beacon, illuminating the path to a disciplined life, enriched by the experiences and lessons that discipline, in its many forms, brings to our lives.

BIO

Joe Pannone, affectionately known as Joey Pinz from his days on the golf course, embodies the essence of discipline in every facet of his remarkable life. Raised in the northeastern U.S. as the son of immigrants, Joe's childhood curiosity evolved into a disciplined approach to question-based learning, a method that has underpinned his journey through life. From shedding over 130 pounds and establishing a successful business that has thrived for over 25 years, to self-teaching computer languages in the dawn of the digital age and earning a pilot's license in his mid-40s, Joe's story is one of relentless determination and disciplined focus.

His achievements span the gamut of human endeavor: maintaining a single-digit golf handicap, completing multiple triathlons, and embarking on an adventurous solo trip from NYC to Italy at the tender age of 10. Joe's resilience and disciplined approach were also crucial in the face of personal loss, leading him to comfort his family and start a foundation in memory of his sister.

However, amidst these diverse and impressive accomplishments, Joe cites fatherhood as his most profound and proudest achievement. Being a dedicated father to two beautiful and smart daughters stands at the pinnacle of his life's work. This role has not only been a source of immense joy but has also deepened his understanding and application of discipline in nurturing, guiding, and learning from his children.

Joe openly acknowledges areas where he seeks to grow and apply more discipline, including philanthropy, financial management, and fostering deeper connections with his extended and European family. His commitment to improvement extends to fitness, community development, and cultivating a more generous spirit towards charity, demonstrating a lifelong commitment to growth and betterment.

Beyond the triumphs and trials, Joe's journey is a testament to the power of discipline as a transformative force. His story is not merely about personal success but about the impactful role of a disciplined life in bettering oneself and contributing positively to the world around us. Through his candid sharing, Joe hopes to inspire others to embrace discipline, confront challenges with resilience, and pursue continuous personal and societal improvement. Among these lessons, he cherishes the journey of fatherhood as the most enriching and rewarding experience of his life, celebrating the beauty and intelligence of his daughters as his crowning accomplishment.